MODERN WORLD NATIONS

AFGHANISTAN
ARGENTINA
AUSTRALIA
AUSTRIA
BAHRAIN
BANGLADESH
BELGIUM
BERMUDA
BOLIVIA
BOSNIA AND
  HERZEGOVINA
BRAZIL
CANADA
CHILE
CHINA
COLOMBIA
COSTA RICA
CROATIA
CUBA
DEMOCRATIC REPUBLIC
  OF THE CONGO
THE DOMINICAN
  REPUBLIC
EGYPT
ENGLAND
ETHIOPIA
FINLAND
FRANCE

REPUBLIC OF GEORGIA
GERMANY
GHANA
GREECE
GUATEMALA
HONDURAS
ICELAND
INDIA
INDONESIA
IRAN
IRAQ
IRELAND
ISRAEL
ITALY
JAMAICA
JAPAN
KAZAKHSTAN
KENYA
KUWAIT
MEXICO
NEPAL
THE NETHERLANDS
NEW ZEALAND
NICARAGUA
NIGERIA
NORTH KOREA
NORWAY

PAKISTAN
PANAMA
PERU
THE PHILIPPINES
POLAND
PORTUGAL
PUERTO RICO
RUSSIA
RWANDA
SAUDI ARABIA
SCOTLAND
SENEGAL
SOUTH AFRICA
SOUTH KOREA
SPAIN
SUDAN
SWEDEN
SYRIA
TAIWAN
THAILAND
TURKEY
UKRAINE
THE UNITED STATES
UZBEKISTAN
VENEZUELA
VIETNAM

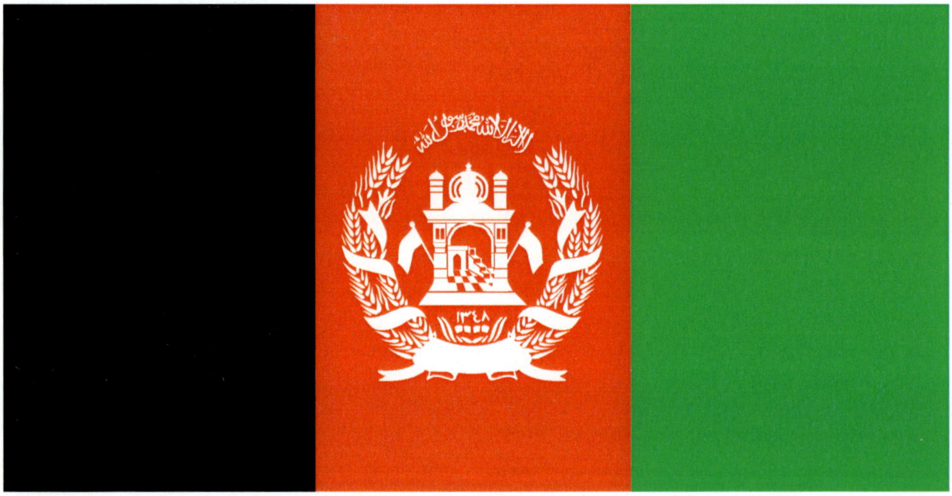

Afghanistan
Third Edition

John F. Shroder Jr.
University of Nebraska, Omaha

and

Jeffrey A. Gritzner
University of Montana

Series Editor
Charles F. Gritzner
South Dakota State University

CHELSEA HOUSE
An Infobase Learning Company

Frontispiece: Flag of Afghanistan

Cover: Kabul, Afghanistan

Afghanistan, Third Edition

Copyright © 2011 by Infobase Learning
All rights reserved. No part of this book may be reproduced or utilized in any form or by any means, electronic or mechanical, including photocopying, recording, or by any information storage or retrieval systems, without permission in writing from the publisher. For information, contact:

Chelsea House
An imprint of Infobase Learning
132 West 31st Street
New York NY 10001

Library of Congress Cataloging-in-Publication Data
Gritzner, Jeffrey A.
  Afghanistan / Jeffrey A. Gritzner and John F. Shroder. -- 3rd ed.
    p. cm. -- (Modern world nations)
  Includes bibliographical references and index.
  ISBN 978-1-60413-941-9 (hardcover : acid-free paper) 1. Afghanistan--Juvenile literature. I. Shroder, John F., 1939- II. Title. III. Series.

  DS351.5.G75 2011
  958.1--dc22
                                       2010036240

Chelsea House books are available at special discounts when purchased in bulk quantities for businesses, associations, institutions, or sales promotions. Please call our Special Sales Department in New York at (212) 967-8800 or (800) 322-8755.

You can find Chelsea House on the World Wide Web at
http://www.chelseahouse.com

Text design by Takeshi Takahashi
Cover design by Alicia Post
Composition by EJB Publishing Services
Cover printed by Yurchak Printing, Landisville, Penn.
Book printed and bound by Yurchak Printing, Landisville, Penn.
Date printed: April 2011
Printed in the United States of America

10 9 8 7 6 5 4 3 2 1

This book is printed on acid-free paper.

All links and Web addresses were checked and verified to be correct at the time of publication. Because of the dynamic nature of the Web, some addresses and links may have changed since publication and may no longer be valid.

Table of Contents

1	Introducing Afghanistan	8
2	Physical Landscapes	15
3	Early History and Culture	27
4	The Age of European Imperialism	39
5	The Soviet Invasion and Its Aftermath	61
6	People and Culture	84
7	Afghanistan's Government and Economy	93
8	Afghanistan Looks Ahead	113
	Facts at a Glance	120
	History at a Glance	123
	Bibliography	126
	Further Reading	127
	Index	129

MODERN WORLD NATIONS

Afghanistan
Third Edition

Introducing Afghanistan

Before the last three decades of warfare there, visitors to Afghanistan often had the feeling that they had stepped into the past. The cultural landscape was almost medieval in character. Massive vertical windmills in the Hari Rud Valley and the mosaics of carefully tended fields and gardens could both have been described by Arab geographers in the seventh century A.D. The traveler would also have seen many *karez* (or *qanat*) that have been known since at least the time of Alexander the Great, over 2,300 years ago. These enormous gently sloping wells were driven into the aquifers near the base of distant mountains, and their presence is indicated by regularly spaced mounds of earth that snake across the landscape. These mounds mark the entrances of the vertical shafts that are used in the excavation and maintenance of the karez.

The visitor would have seen many picturesque walled villages with beehive-domed dwellings and bazaars (markets) enlivened by the sounds of artisans at work and the pungent odors of spices and herbs. One could visit an encampment of the Pashtun (or Pushtun) Kuchi nomads, with their black goat's-hair tents and often-complaining camels. The name *Pashtun* is widely used to identify individuals or groups associated with the many Pashtu-speaking tribes of Afghanistan and Pakistan.

Proud, self-confident, and hospitable, Afghans are a people who have defied colonization. Through time, they have defended their freedom in the face of the most powerful armies on Earth. In 1952, in his book *Beyond the High Himalaya*, Supreme Court Justice William O. Douglas wrote:

> We of the West have all the rudiments of civilization, all the dividends of a mounting standard of living. But the Afghans—one thousand years behind us in many respects—have a warmth of human relations that is often missing all the way from New York City to San Francisco.

Ironically, in recent decades, both internal strife and the imposition of outside "civilization" or "democracy" upon the people of Afghanistan have contributed to the erosion of the "warmth of human relations" so admired by Justice Douglas and many others who know this land and its people. The people of Afghanistan always have been the implacable foes of the outside invader. The present-day situation of incessant strife is no different than it has been countless times in the past when outside forces tried to control them.

The sturdiness of Afghanistan's people is matched by the country's natural landscape. Rugged mountains and extensive desert plains dominate Afghanistan's physical geography. More than one hundred peaks in the region's towering Pamir Knot—often called the "Roof of the World"—rise above 20,000 feet (6,100 meters), including many that are located in Afghanistan. The country's highest mountain, Nowshak, rises to 24,557 feet

(7,485 meters), on the Pakistan border—higher than any peak in the Western Hemisphere. Several peaks in the central ranges exceed 14,000 feet (4,270 meters) in elevation. The region is geologically active and the mountains are still growing.

This activity also contributes to frequent seismic (earthquake) activity that poses a constant threat to life and property. For example, in the 150 years that records have been kept, there have been more major earthquakes in southern Badakhshan Province than in any other place in the world—more than 21 earthquakes of magnitude 7 or greater. Despite their geologically young age, these mountains have been deeply scoured by glaciers and running water. Precipitation is greatest in the highlands. Melting snow and mountain rains feed rivers, such as the Helmand. Its waters, as well as those of other streams, erode and deepen valleys, transport and deposit the sediment on the broad plains, and irrigate the semiarid lowlands.

One river-scoured gorge, in particular, has become famous. Khyber Pass, located in Pakistan on Afghanistan's eastern border, cuts through the east end of the Safed Koh (or Spin Ghar in Pashto) range. Historically, it was one of the world's most important land routes, linking the Mediterranean region and Southwest Asia with the subcontinent of India and present-day Pakistan.

Southern Afghanistan's physical landscape is dominated by semiarid plains and parched deserts. The extensive sand dunes of the Registan region cover vast areas there. Northern Afghanistan, along the Amu Dar'ya (Amu River) boundary with Tajikistan, Uzbekistan, and Turkmenistan, similarly has wide expanses of sand dunes that are produced by the strong winds and extensive sands brought out of the mountains of Badakhshan.

Mountain climates vary greatly. Upwind sides can be quite wet, whereas downwind sides can be extremely dry. Temperatures can be scorching on the desert floor at the foot of a mountain, whereas glaciers and permanent snowfields cap the mountain's crest. In general, however, the country's summers

Introducing Afghanistan   11

The landscape of Afghanistan is composed of rugged mountains, deeply cut valleys, and broad alluvial plains. Pictured here are the Hindu Kush mountain range. This area of northeastern Afghanistan is home to some of the world's highest mountains, including Nowshak, the nation's tallest mountain at 24,557 feet (7,485 meters).

are hot and dry and winters are cold, with heavy snowfall in the mountains. Average precipitation is roughly 13 inches (330 millimeters), with the extremes ranging from 36 inches (914 millimeters) in the Salang Pass area to 2 inches (51 millimeters) in the southwestern deserts. Winds tend to blow from the north and northwest. During the summer, they are hot and often howling—velocities can reach 115 miles per hour (185 kilometers per hour)—and accompanied by huge dust storms. The summer winds of the southwestern deserts are known as the *bad-i-sad-u-bist ruz*—the "wind of 120 days." Vast areas of Afghanistan are covered with thick deposits of wind-blown dust, or loess, which can occur as blanket deposits or be eroded over time to form steep-sided loess hills that can be aligned with dominant wind directions.

The area now occupied by Afghanistan entered documented history during the Bronze Age, about 4,000 years ago. The earliest Persian (Iranian) chronicles suggest that the region to the north and west of the Helmand River was dominated by nomadic, Indo-European-speaking Scythians. Eastern Afghanistan was dominated by Dravidian speakers associated with the Indus civilization, located to the east in present-day Pakistan and India. During the Aryan migrations of the second and first millennia B.C., Iranian tribes settled in the region and established several important kingdoms—including Bactria, home of the prophet Zoroaster.

With the expansion of the Achaemenid Empire in the sixth century B.C., Afghanistan included seven important satrapies, or provinces: Gandhara (the Jalalabad area), Bactria, Merv, Herat, Sattagydia (the southeastern lowlands), Arachosia (Kandahar), and Zaranka (Sistan). The satrapies were, in a sense, the foundation of modern Afghanistan. The country has long been (and continues to be) sharply divided along provincial and ethnic lines.

The name *Afghanistan* simply means "Land of the Afghan." In the past, the term *Afghan* referred to Pashtun nomads. The term was then expanded to include all citizens of modern Afghanistan. There are many translations of the term *Afghan*. Some describe an arrogant or unruly people—terms applied by others in reference to the people who today bear the name. Some refer to a people courageous or free. Another interpretation refers to the spiritual station of the soul, characterized by one who has achieved purity. It is not known for certain when or why the name was first used, but in all likelihood it was first used by British explorers in the nineteenth century.

Introducing Afghanistan 13

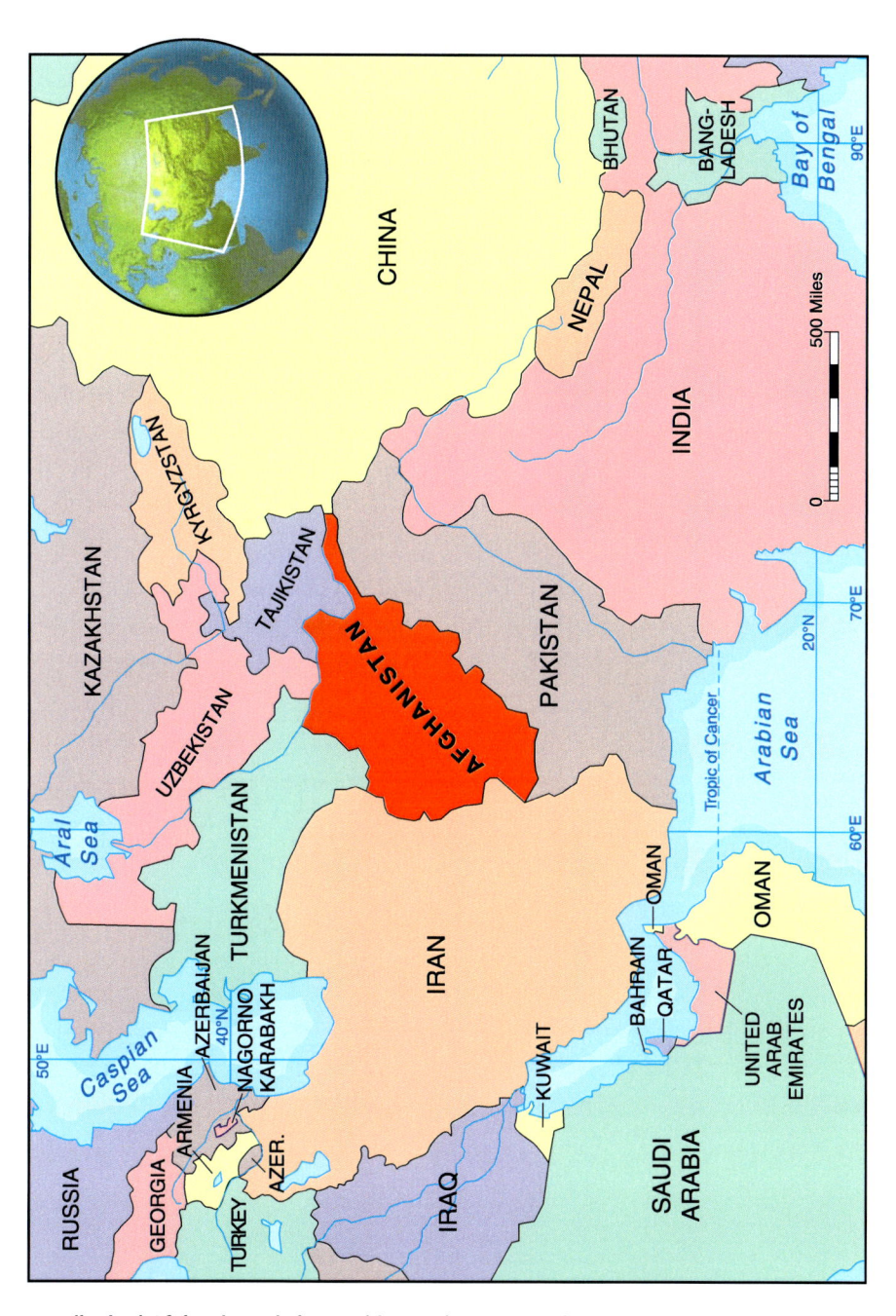

Landlocked Afghanistan is located in southern Central Asia and shares borders with the former Soviet Republics of Turkmenistan, Uzbekistan, and Tajikistan to the north, Iran to the west, Pakistan to the south and east, and China to the northeast.

Afghanistan is located in southern Central Asia. In some respects, it suffers from its inland location. Lack of direct access to the global sea has limited its contact with other places and peoples. Isolation also has restricted trade with other lands. Its neighbors are Turkmenistan, Uzbekistan, and Tajikistan to the north (all former Soviet Republics); the Xinjiang region of China (through the Wakhan Corridor—a narrow strip of land extending eastward between Tajikistan and Pakistan) to the northeast; Pakistan to the south and east; and Iran to the west. With a total area of 252,092 square miles (652,915 square kilometers), Afghanistan is slightly smaller than Texas. It is also located roughly within the same latitudes as Texas, and both have resident populations of more than 20 million people.

In 2001, as a result of the tragic events associated with terrorist attacks on the United States, Afghanistan was catapulted onto the global stage. American writer Ambrose Bierce once said, "War is God's way of teaching Americans geography." Sadly, this seems to be true about interest in and knowledge of Afghanistan. As a result of the military action involving the United States and other countries that began in late 2001, people throughout the world have become much more aware of this quaint, traditional, isolated—yet important—country.

CHAPTER

2

Physical Landscapes

Few countries in the world have a more challenging natural landscape than does Afghanistan. It is a country of towering mountains and broad desert plains. The rugged land has divided the country's regions and people—a chief factor contributing to Afghanistan's long history of regional and ethnic conflict. Ruggedness, combined with aridity, affects the economy as well. Not much of the land is suited to the raising of crops, a condition made even more troublesome by the country's lack of precipitation. Afghanistan also suffers from its landlocked condition, an interior location with no direct access to the sea. This chapter discusses the country's weather and climate, landforms, water features, and ecosystems. Each element plays an important role in Afghanistan's physical, historical, and cultural geography.

CLIMATE

There are three principal types of climate in Afghanistan: a midlatitude steppe and desert climate in the north, a variable highland climate in the eastern and central mountains, and a low-latitude tropical steppe and desert climate in the south. The relatively high elevation and continental character of Afghanistan result in significant annual and daily temperature changes. Kabul, at an elevation of 5,955 feet (1,815 meters), typically experiences a winter temperature range of 58° to −6°F (14° to −21°C), and a summer range of 101° to 58°F (38° to 14°C). A 50°F (10°C) temperature change from sunrise to early afternoon is possible.

Most precipitation arrives with the eastward penetration of moisture-laden air masses during the winter and spring. The average annual precipitation is 13 inches (330 millimeters). Summers and autumns are hot and dry. Predictably, humidity is low throughout most of the year. During summer and autumn afternoons, humidity often drops below 25 percent. Although levels of precipitation are lower in the south, the southern regions often receive some summer rains from the northward penetration of the Indian monsoon. During the summer and autumn, strong winds, the *bad-i-sad-u-bist ruz*, sweep south out of the interior of Asia through a gap between the Paropamisus (Selseleh-ye) range in northwestern Afghanistan and towering ranges to the west in neighboring Iran and Turkmenistan.

CLIMATE CHANGE

Thousands of years ago, the great basin of the Helmand River in the southwest of Afghanistan was inundated by a huge lake; ancient civilizations prospered in this well-watered environment. Natural climate change, having nothing to do with greenhouse gases or any other human-produced pollutants, caused this lake to dry up into a series of small *hamuns*, or temporary lakes, that now periodically disappear altogether in times of drought. In the past four decades, these droughts have been increasing in duration and severity. The future for Afghanistan's climate does not look good.

Models of future climate change in Afghanistan are based on the most likely global circulation patterns, wherein observed climate warming causes an increase in size and change in position of the vertical air-circulation Hadley and Ferrel cells in the atmosphere. When these changed cells are applied to the usual climate patterns of Afghanistan, some potentially disturbing patterns emerge. The best scientific predictions by the National Oceanic and Atmospheric Administration (NOAA) are that southern Afghanistan will continue to get drier in the next 20 years, exactly as has been seen in recent decades. On the other hand, these same predictions indicate that northern Afghanistan may become somewhat wetter, which would be very good news if it does happen. Such increases in moisture from westerly winter storms and in summertime cloudiness have caused glaciers to grow in the nearby Karakoram Himalaya of Pakistan, but have yet to show up in Afghanistan.

LAND FEATURES

Afghanistan is a land of many contrasts. The natural landscape is composed of mountains, deeply cut valleys, and broad alluvial plains (land built from stream deposition). The mountains are composed mainly of ancient sediments deposited under marine conditions. As segments of Earth's single land mass, known as Gondwanaland, moved northward during the late Jurassic and Cretaceous periods (163 to 65 million years ago), these sediments were compressed and thrust upward (as well as being intruded by vast amounts of melted igneous rocks) to form the great Alpine-Himalayan mountain belt. The belt remains geologically active, and earthquakes with magnitudes of 6.5 to 7.5 on the Richter scale are common. Nearly 10,000 people were killed by severe earthquakes in February 1998,

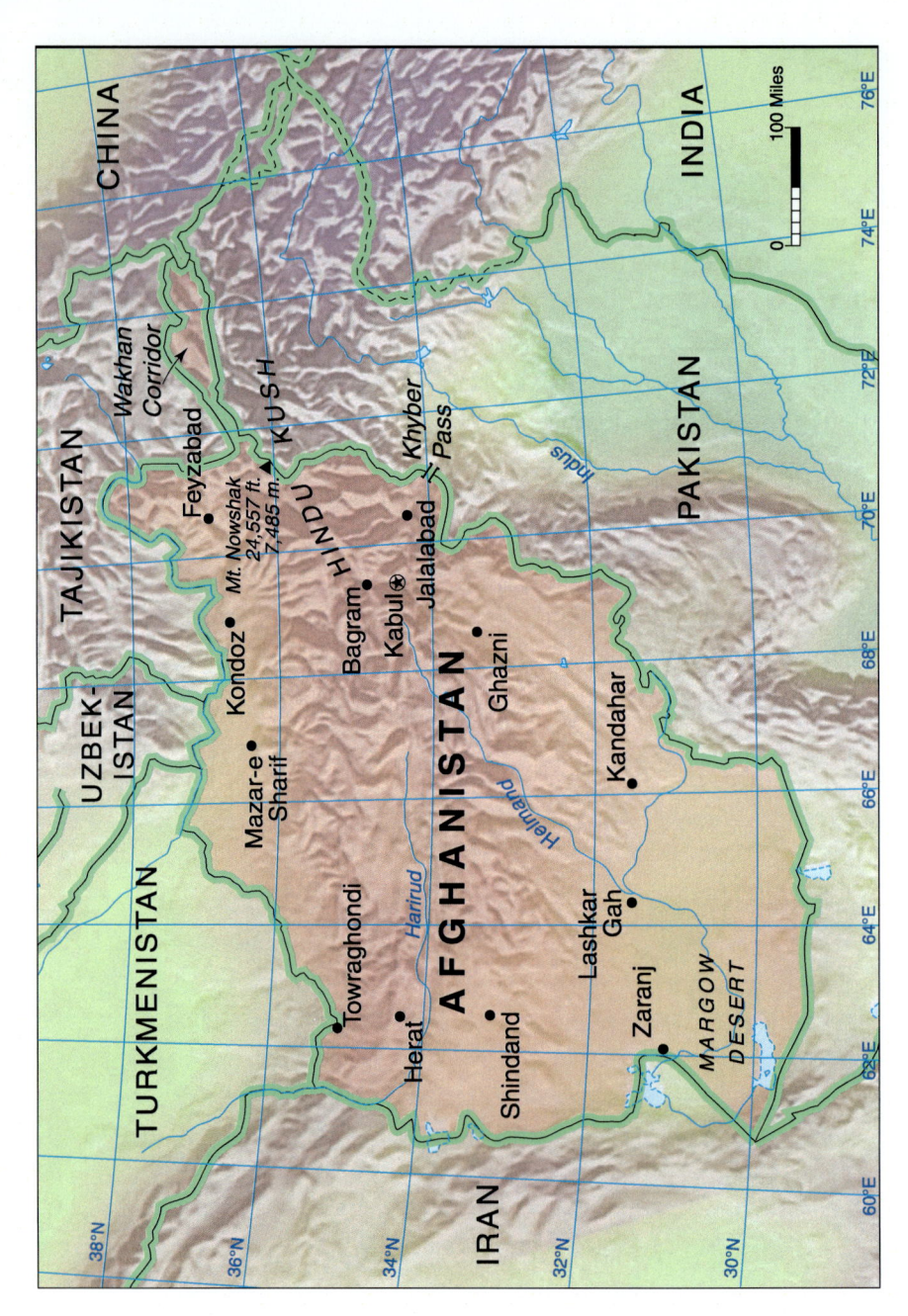

As depicted on this map of Afghanistan, mountains dominate the northern three quarters of the country. The primary range is the Hindu Kush, which stretches east to west, gradually declining in elevation as it approaches the border with Iran.

and another 2,000 lost their lives in a devastating quake on the slopes of the Hindu Kush range in March 2002.

The Hindu Kush system extends westward from the Pamir Knot for some 700 miles (1,127 kilometers), almost reaching the Iranian border. Some simply regard the Safed Koh as a westerly extension of the Hindu Kush, rather than as a separate range. Among the other major ranges of the Hindu Kush complex are Koh-e Baba and the Turkestan Mountains. The mountains effectively divide Afghanistan into two regions, with the northern lowlands being smaller in area than those to the south. Within the highlands are many long, narrow basins—commonly the result of grabens (depressed segments of earth bounded by faults on at least two sides). Extensive rolling plains covered with sagebrush and sand dunes occur near the Amu Dar'ya (Amu River) in the north, the Helmand River in the south, around Kabul, and in Herat Province. The geological structures of Afghanistan are associated with a considerable variety and wealth of minerals. The rich store of mineral resources includes the hydrocarbons natural gas, petroleum, and coal. Among the metals are stores of copper, iron, gold, lead, zinc, and lithium. The country also has deposits of talc, barite, sulfur, and salt, and a considerable variety of precious and semiprecious stones, including emeralds, rubies, topaz, aquamarine, tourmaline, kunzite, and lapis lazuli.

Historically, Afghanistan's best known and perhaps most important landform feature has been the famous Khyber Pass, which lies five miles (8 kilometers) east within Pakistan. This narrow, steep-sided pass snakes for some 30 miles (48.2 kilometers) through the Safed Koh Mountains on the border between Afghanistan and Pakistan. Its highest point is about 3,500 feet (1,067 meters), well below the elevation where long and heavy winter snowfall occurs. Although only about 12 feet (4 meters) wide in places, Khyber is one of the world's most famous mountain passes. It was a major link between the riches of India and Pakistan to the east, and Persia, Mesopotamia, and other wealthy and powerful lands to the west.

Both archaeology and history amply document the importance of the Khyber Pass over a period of at least 3,500 years. Conquering forces and caravans of traders found it to be the shortest and easiest land route between east and west. The Greek conqueror Alexander the Great may have been the first recorded user of the pass (or another nearby) when, in 326 B.C., his army marched through a pass in this region on its way to India. More than a thousand years later, Persian and Tartar troops stormed through the pass as they carried the Islamic faith into the Indus Valley and on to India. Mongols from the steppes of inner Asia also used the pass to invade and place their cultural imprint on Pakistan and India. More recently, the pass played an important role in nineteenth-century Afghan wars fought by the British. Today, a paved highway and traditional caravan route follow the pass, linking the cities of Kabul in Afghanistan and Peshawar in Pakistan.

WATER FEATURES

Most of Afghanistan's important rivers rise in the central mountains. Because they are heavily dependent on rainfall and melting snow, maximum flow is typically in the spring and early summer. During late summer, autumn, and winter, some rivers, such as the Khash Rud, are reduced to a series of unconnected pools in the streambed. There are four major river systems in Afghanistan: the Amu Dar'ya in the north, the Helmand-Arghandab in the south, the Kabul in the east, and the Hari Rud in the west.

The Nile-sized Amu Dar'ya flows along the Afghan borders with Tajikistan, Uzbekistan, and Turkmenistan for 680 miles (1,094 kilometers) before turning northwest toward the Aral Sea. It is important for transportation as well as for irrigation. Among its major tributaries are the Kowkcheh and Kunduz. The waters of many tributaries are diverted for irrigation before reaching the Amu Dar'ya.

The Helmand River system drains roughly 40 percent of Afghanistan. The river rises in the Koh-e Baba Range and flows for some 800 miles (1,287 kilometers), first in a southwesterly direction and then northward, emptying into the Sistan Basin of Iran. As it flows southward, the Helmand is joined by the Arghandab near the city of Lashkar Gah, where irrigation canal outtakes originally built with American foreign aid water the oases of Nadi Ali and Marjah. The Arghandab rises to the north of Kandahar and, before joining the Helmand, loses much of its water to irrigated agriculture. The Kabul River is a tributary of the Indus River system. From its headwaters near Unai Pass west of Kabul, it flows some 225 miles (362 kilometers) in an easterly direction through the Kabul Valley, Daruntah Gorge, and the Jalalabad Plains before entering the Peshawar Valley north of the Khyber Pass and joining the mighty Indus River of Pakistan.

The Hari Rud flows almost due west from the Hesar Range in the central Hindu Kush. After passing through Herat and Eslam Qal'eh, the Hari Rud turns northward, forming roughly 100 miles (161 kilometers) of the Afghan-Iranian border before entering Turkmenistan. A second major river in western Afghanistan, the Morghab, similarly flows northward into Turkmenistan.

Many small streams and some lakes are intermittent; that is, they flow or contain water only after periods of precipitation or following spring snowmelt. In an arid land, water is precious. Streams and groundwater are the source of both the domestic water supply and that used for irrigation—the lifeblood of Afghanistan's economy. But the lack of water is a major problem in both rural and urban areas due to scarcity, mismanagement, and war-damaged water systems. The country uses less than one-third of its potential 2,648 million cubic feet (75,000 million cubic meters) of water resources, and only about 20 percent of Afghans nationwide have ever had access to safe drinking water.

SOILS

Many elements come together to create soils. The most important factors in soil formation are parent material (the rock material from which the soil is created), climate, plant and animal life, landforms, and the length of time over which these various elements have been at work. The soils of Afghanistan fall into two main categories. One is typical of dry climates; it is low in organic matter and is affected by the processes of calcification and salinization (accumulation of calcium and salt). The other category, alluvium, is found in active slopes, basins, and flood plains; these soils are usually young or undeveloped. Factors of soil formation are important simply because these elements determine a soil's fertility.

Even though nearly two-thirds of the country's economy is based on agriculture, only about 12 percent of its land is suited to raising crops. Soil degradation (the process of soils becoming less fertile) can occur through erosion, the loss of vegetation cover as occurs in overgrazing and firewood cutting, salt accumulation through irrigation, and other processes. Afghanistan has experienced widespread loss of its soil resources over thousands of years of poor land management. This is particularly true of the dry-climate soils as they are highly susceptible to the processes of salinization and water-logging. Because soil formation takes a long time, the wise management and rebuilding of soil resources is an issue of considerable importance.

In fact most of Afghanistan has experienced environmental deterioration and the loss of soils for many centuries. As a result, the country is now experiencing widespread desertification, or the process of once-fertile land becoming desert. Deforestation, deshrubification (the pulling up of shrubs for fuel), soil salinization, and wind and water erosion are all parts of the human-induced processes of desertification. With its climate changing toward drier conditions and desertification increasing, Afghanistan becomes progressively less productive and livable for its already sorely stressed population.

Physical Landscapes

Woodlands once occupied a large part of Afghanistan, but according to recent studies by the United Nations, forests now cover just 2.5 percent of the country. Poplars, such as these in the Bamiyan Province of northcentral Afghanistan, once thrived in a majority of the country's rugged terrain.

ECOSYSTEMS AND WILDLIFE

Afghanistan's natural vegetation has suffered from centuries of abuse. In the distant past, woodlands or dense grasses covered much of the country. Today, forests occupy a much smaller area than in the past, and many former grassland regions are now semidesert, or in some other degraded form. Some 40 percent of the already sparse forests were cut down in the past three decades of war so that only 2 to 3 percent of the country remains forested. Much of the deforestation has been accomplished by timber "mafia," because so much money can be made in this land of limited forest resources.

Elevation also plays a key role in determining Afghanistan's ecosystems. With declining elevation, highland alpine tundra gives way to dense forests of needle-leaf, coniferous evergreen species. At still lower elevations, mixed woodlands and grasslands thrive. They, in turn, finally give way to semiarid steppe grasslands.

Five major ecosystems dominate Afghanistan's landscapes. Alpine tundra occurs at high elevations, above the tree line and below the level of permanent snow and ice. Its natural vegetation is composed of hardy grasses, small flowering plants, and stunted shrubs. Snow leopards, rare Siberian tigers, and brown bears occur in this harsh and remote natural environment. The great Marco Polo sheep live high in the Wakhan Corridor panhandle to the northeast.

Below the alpine tundra, warmer temperatures allow the growth of trees. This is the zone of mountain forests, which once occupied about 45 percent of the country. Vegetation includes pine, spruce, fir, and larch trees. Forests abound with animal life, including lynx and other large cats. There also are wolves, foxes, ferrets, weasels, otters, martens, and badgers, as well as deer and wild sheep.

A semidesert ecosystem occurs in the cool northern lowland plains. Vegetation includes grasses and a variety of robust annual and perennial plants and shrubs. Wildlife includes a variety of birds; small animals such as hedgehogs, hares, and gophers; and larger carnivores such as wolves, jackals, and hyenas.

On the plains located south and west of the central highlands, midlatitude steppe (short-grass) grasslands flourish. Broadleaf trees commonly grow along watercourses and in a few other locations favorable for their growth. Animal species include gazelles, wild pigs, jackals, and hyenas.

Finally, semidesert conditions prevail in the warm, semi-arid southern part of Afghanistan. Vegetation is composed mainly of short grasses, which are often scattered rather than growing as a solid carpet. There are also a few woody perennials that are well adapted to the region's aridity. Wildlife is similar to that in the short-grass steppes but also includes some fauna common to India, such as the mongoose, leopard, cheetah, and macaque (a monkey).

The highly mountainous country of Afghanistan contains a variety of ecological habitats. Although recent events have severely reduced wildlife populations, the country's complex ecology continues to support a remarkable diversity of wildlife. All large wildlife in Afghanistan is hunted mercilessly, and a number of species are close to extinction.

In addition to the carnivores mentioned previously, Afghanistan is also home to marbled polecats, rhesus monkeys, shrews, Cape hares, squirrels, gophers, and groundhogs. There are also Indian-crested porcupines; several species of rats, gerbils, voles, and mice; and a variety of bat species.

There are believed to be approximately 390 species of birds in Afghanistan, and several species are hunted for sport and food. Important game birds include partridges, pheasants, and quail. Some 80 species of wild pigeons and doves are also found, and large numbers of waterfowl arrive during the course of their spring and autumn migrations. Among the waterfowl are several species of ducks, grebes, geese, pelicans, and swans. A few rare and endangered Siberian cranes once had a migration stopover at the Ab-i-Stada Lake between Ghazni and Kandahar in the last quarter of the twentieth century, but recent drought may have eliminated that small population from Afghanistan. There are also many shorebirds such as snipes, plovers, herons, storks, and cranes. The Baluch people of the marshy Sistan region are specialists in hunting and fishing. From their reed or dugout watercraft, they also snare birds with the same nets that they use for fishing.

There are many birds of prey, including eagles, hawks, falcons, and vultures. Among the smaller and more common birds are larks, warblers, sparrows, flycatchers, and swallows. Crows, magpies, and jays are familiar species common in some areas of human habitation. Afghanistan also has large land turtles and a variety of frogs and toads. There are a dozen or so species of lizards, including the monitor lizard, which grows to a length of six feet (almost two meters). Among the many snakes are several that are deadly poisonous. They include two species of cobra (the brightly banded and deadly krait) and several vipers. Scorpions, some of which are poisonous, are also found throughout the dry lands of the country.

Fish abound in the watercourses of Afghanistan but are not widely used as a food resource. This may be due to the considerable distance most people live from freshwater and the fact that fish meat is highly perishable. German brown trout occur in streams north of the Hindu Kush, and rainbow trout have been released in the Salang and Panjshir rivers. Four varieties of carp were introduced from China in the late 1960s, in the hope that fish would become a more important source of food for many of the country's poor, rural people. In the warmer waters of the Amu Dar'ya, a form of European catfish, the *laka*, often grows to more than seven feet (two meters) in length. Freshwater crabs occur throughout the country.

While many insects play important roles as pollinators or biological controls in gardens and fields, many others spread disease, attack crops, or otherwise cause annoyance. Mosquitoes, flies, and biting gnats occur throughout the country. Fleas, ticks, lice, and roaches are common pests throughout the lowlands. Insect-borne diseases are becoming increasingly widespread. Malaria is becoming increasingly severe and widespread, as are diarrhea and other diseases associated with contaminated water supplies. They contribute significantly to the declining life expectancy of Afghans, which currently is one of the world's shortest.

3

Early History and Culture

Afghanistan has a long and complex history. Without an understanding of the country's past, it is impossible to understand many conditions existing today. For that reason, three chapters are devoted to the topic. This chapter discusses the country's earliest peoples and their way of life up to the fifteenth century. Chapter 4, "The Age of European Imperialism," covers the period from the nineteenth century to the 1970s, during which European influence was strongly imprinted on Afghanistan. Finally, Chapter 5 discusses the country's recent history and the impact of the Soviet invasion and its aftermath.

PREHISTORY

Ancient Paleolithic (Old Stone Age) people probably roamed what is now Afghanistan as early as 100,000 years ago. Certainly Mousterian

(Neanderthal) populations were present in the area 50,000 to 30,000 years ago, during the Middle Paleolithic period (Middle Stone Age). Among the archaeological sites yielding evidence of Middle Paleolithic Mousterian occupation are Dara-e Kur in Badakhshan Province and Ghar-e Mordeh Gusfand in Ghowr Province. The Middle Paleolithic was a period during which accumulated knowledge grew rapidly. People learned to make better tools and weapons that, in turn, made it possible for them to exploit a broad range of plant and animal resources. Their most important tool was fire. Combined with more effective weapons, it contributed to the extinction of many species. The environment, too, underwent change as a result of the widespread use of fire as a hunting and clearing tool. Many wooded areas were changed into the grasslands that cover widespread areas of Afghanistan even today.

Afghanistan is located within the region of the world that is most often associated with the beginning of the Neolithic (New Stone Age) Revolution. Surprisingly, perhaps, this revolution, although bearing the name *stone*, is more involved with the dawn of plant and animal domestication. When domestication first occurred in the region, perhaps some 11,000 years ago, people were able to raise crops and tend herds, rather than gathering and hunting to provide for their needs. Baluchistan was a particularly important early center of cereal cultivation. The crops included two types of barley, two kinds of wheat, and dates. The resultant crop and livestock combinations allowed societies to control their food supplies. A greater and more reliable food supply also eventually contributed to the emergence of the earliest urban centers, such as Mundigak and Deh Morasi Ghundai near Kandahar.

The cultural geographer can learn much by studying early peoples. As the environment changed, society itself changed in many ways, and the transition from rural nomadic living to city life required a completely different set of social, economic, technological, and other "survival" skills.

With farming and grazing, Afghanistan's environmental systems began to change. Specifically, they evolved to serve the needs of people and societies that had abandoned hunting and gathering and had become involved in agriculture, trade, and other more sedentary forms of livelihood. Grasslands and woodlands were converted to agricultural fields, and open grasslands became pasturelands for domesticated livestock. Grazing livestock, agricultural expansion, and the use of wood for construction and fuel further greatly reduced natural vegetative cover.

Afghanistan provides the environmental geographer with an extensive "laboratory" in which to study human impact on the natural environment. As natural vegetation cover decreased as a result of human activity, for example, the atmospheric moisture available for precipitation decreased (because of reduced plant transpiration). With reduced vegetation, soil temperatures increased, soil-moisture content was altered, soil ecology was simplified, and soil structure was modified. This list of changes may seem extremely complex—and it is. However, it illustrates how very complicated natural systems can be, and how a single human act—in this case, reducing natural vegetation cover—can affect other environmental elements. In this example, the quality of soil declined greatly. In fact, conditions favorable for the regeneration of many of Afghanistan's soils and native plants may no longer exist. Agricultural productivity has been reduced, as has the quality of grazing lands, and reduced moisture infiltration and unobstructed runoff have increased flooding that, in turn, affects settlement and other land-use activities in the flood-prone lowlands.

ANCIENT HISTORY

Historically, Afghanistan was the meeting place of three major ecological and cultural areas: Central Asia to the north, the Indian subcontinent to the east, and the Middle East to the west. Located between these centers of powerful civilizations,

Afghanistan often fell prey to outside forces. During the mid-first millennium B.C., the region became the home of important eastern Iranian kingdoms, such as Bactria, and it was incorporated into the Achaemenid Empire of the western Iranians during the sixth century B.C.

By the first millennium B.C., agriculture and other forms of environmental alteration had been practiced in the region for thousands of years. Erosion, caused by the removal of vegetation, soil compaction, and salinization, was severe. Good farmland was reduced, and surface water quality was affected. Many formerly productive lowland basin lakes, such as Namakzar, became playas—unproductive desert basins that only occasionally hold water. While water from canals and near-surface wells continued to support cultivation in many areas, the deterioration of water quality in other areas encouraged the excavation of underground canals, or karez. In northern Afghanistan, they may date from the fifth century B.C. It is believed that they were excavated by members of an itinerant guild of specialists. A mid-nineteenth century traveler, Evliya Efendi, wrote:

> The aqueduct-men by their skill in mathematics dig through mountains to the depth of seventy or eighty yards, and conduct the water four or five journies distance. Every hundred paces they open a well-mouth, over which they put a windsail to admit air to the water, till it arrives at the place they desire it to be brought to, by levelling. It is a wonderful art. These men dig here and there, and feign to be consulting from whence water shall be brought, or to where it shall be conducted. They are all Albanese.

Most karez are gently sloping, nearly horizontal wells that tap the groundwater from sources that occur in distant alluvial fans found at the base of mountains. Water is then transported (by gravity flow) in underground aqueducts (canals) to an

Afghanistan stood at the crossroads of several ancient empires and thus was subject to invasions from these foreign powers. Watchtowers such as this one in the Bamiyan Valley of north-central Afghanistan helped ensure that local residents were warned before these outside forces entered the region. Unfortunately, the Taliban has destroyed many of these ancient sites in recent years.

agricultural village. This technology had many applications in the past. In some instances, karez were fed by diverted streams and carried the water underground to its destination. The karez were able to deliver large quantities of uncontaminated water to upslope soils unaffected by salinization, waterlogging, or flooding. Temples often received water from particular streams considered to be sacred. The karez digging guilds were also called upon occasionally to divert water from cities under siege.

In the semiarid lowlands of Afghanistan, pastoral nomadism emerged from village-based pastoralism. The increased range of livestock grazing permitted the exploitation of increasingly sparse vegetation over vast areas. As environmental systems became less productive, many nomads joined settled Afghan populations in an increasing number of towns and cities—a trend that continues to the present day.

Hellenistic (Greek) influences intensified in Afghanistan following Alexander III of Macedon's (Alexander the Great) victory over the Achaemenid emperor Darius III in 331 B.C. and the emergence of the Seleucid Empire. The Seleucid period in Afghanistan is complex, owing to considerable conflict, displacement, and political change. Among the most prominent groups were Greco-Bactrians; the Mauryan Empire under Ashoka (296–237 B.C.); the nomadic Saka (Scythians); and the Yüeh-chih (or Kushan nomads). Much of the turmoil ended with the expansion of the Parthian Empire under Mithradates I around 171 B.C. It was a powerful empire that prevented further eastward expansion of the Roman Empire.

Afghanistan was also the home of important elements of the later Sassanian Empire, such as the Hephthalites. As the influence of Sassanian kings yielded to the competing interests of religious leaders and bureaucrats, the empire declined. The void was filled by the arrival of Islam, and a succession of Arab caliphs (successors of Muhammad as spiritual leaders of Islam) that began in A.D. 652.

THE EARLY ISLAMIC PERIOD

Islam reached Afghanistan during the mid-seventh century. Turmoil, however, would persist as control continued to change hands frequently. With the decline of the Abbasid Caliphate in the ninth century A.D., Afghanistan fell under the control of the Tahirid Emirate and later the Saffarid Emirate. During the tenth century, it was associated with the powerful Samanid and Ghaznavid emirates—the latter an indigenous (native) dynasty

Early History and Culture

established by Nasir ad-Dawlah Subuktigin, a Turkish general who overthrew his Samanid master in A.D. 977. Under the leadership of his son Yamin ad-Dawlah Mahmud, the Ghaznavids created an empire extending from Kurdistan to Kashmir, and from the Amu Dar'ya (Oxus River of antiquity) to the Ganges (Ganga) River. Mahmud was a patron of the arts and literature and was said to have had 900 resident scholars, including the scientist-historian al-Biruni and the poet Firdousi, in his House of Learning.

Afghanistan was later incorporated into the extensive Seljuk Sultanate. Divisions formed within the sultanate, resulting in the emergence of a separate Seljuk Sultanate of Merv in Central Asia. It, in turn, fell into anarchy upon the revolt of its Ghuzz mercenaries. During the thirteenth century, Afghanistan was included in the Shahdom of Khwarezm, a state then devastated by the merciless campaigns of Genghis Khan and the Mongols in 1220 and 1221. During the fourteenth century, Mongol authority in Afghanistan yielded to several native provincial governments, such as the Kart Emirate, and then to the forces of the Turkish noble Timur (Tamerlane). Effective Timurid control extended through the fifteenth century.

CULTURAL CONTRIBUTIONS OF EARLY AFGHANISTAN

The many kingdoms and empires that controlled the region at various times made important contributions to religion, literature, architecture, agriculture, gardening, and crafts.

It was from this region that the prophet Zoroaster (ca. 628–ca. 551 B.C.) introduced the strict dualism of good and evil principles, light and dark, and angels and devils that so profoundly influenced Hebrew beliefs, Greek thought, and Christianity. It was also from Afghanistan, chiefly from the first through the fifth centuries A.D., that Mahayana Buddhism traveled eastward over the ancient Silk Route to Mongolia, China, Korea, and Japan. (Ironically, the Buddhist Mongol hordes of Genghis Khan followed the same route westward

Yamin ad-Dawlah Mahmud, or Mahmud of Ghazni, ruled the Ghaznavid Empire from A.D. 997 to 1030. At the center of this empire, which covered most of present-day Afghanistan, Iran, and parts of India and Pakistan, was the city of Ghazni. The tomb of Mahmud of Ghazni, pictured here, is the only structure that remains from the ancient city.

in the 1220 and 1221 campaigns that ravaged Afghanistan.) Since the arrival of Islam, Afghanistan has been associated with Sufi mysticism—a vehicle for seeking God through personal experience and achieving momentary union with God. Among the well-known Afghan Sufis were Sana'i (died 1131) of Ghazni and Rumi (1207–1273), born in Balkh and founder of the Mawlawiya Dervishes.

Herat, Balkh, Kabul, and Ghazni were prominent literary centers in Afghanistan. The court compositions of the Achaemenid Empire (559–30 B.C.) established literary traditions echoed in later works, such as the *Shahname* ("Book of Kings") by Firdousi (died ca. A.D. 1020). Firdousi was the most prominent of the 400 poets who resided in the court of Mahmud of Ghazni. The *Shahname* ranks among the world's great epic poems.

In addition to the more or less official manuals of the imperial court, there were historical romances, urban histories, and compilations concerned with ethics. But the region is best known for its excellent poetry. Much of the poetry was of considerable length—the *Shahname*, for example, was composed of 60,000 rhyming couplets. That of the mathematician and philosopher Omar Khayyám (died 1123) is representative of a shorter verse-form, the popular *ruba'i*:

> A Book of Verses underneath the Bough,
> A Jug of Wine, a Loaf of Bread—and Thou
> Beside me singing in the Wilderness—
> O, Wilderness were Paradise enow!

Prominent among later Afghan authors was Jami (1414–1492), a poet, scholar, and mystic who wrote at least 46 major works in the fields of lyrical and romantic narrative poetry, grammar, music, mysticism, the lives of the Sufi saints, and Koranic studies. In Afghanistan, the mysticism and the polished elegance of Persian poetry later developed in tandem with works in the more direct language of the tribal poets. For them, prowess in warfare against infidel (non-Muslim) foreigners was a favorite theme:

> Whoever is a Moslem, whoever is of good faith in Islam
> ... goes to the sacred war, gives up his life and goods for the law of the Holy Prophet, and is not afraid of the infidels.

Other popular themes were love, jealousy, religion, and folklore. Today most Afghans, literate or nonliterate, consider themselves to be poets—and prior to the Soviet military incursions of the late 1970s, a remarkable literary renaissance was taking place in Afghanistan. It found expression in the many journals and other publications of the Pushtu Tulena (Afghan Academy), the Afghan Encyclopedia Society, the Anjoman Tarikh-e Afghanistan (Afghan Historical Society), and other scholarly societies.

Several architectural innovations were established within the ancient empires of the region—including the arch, barrel vault, and dome—that strongly influenced the architecture of Greece, Rome, and the modern world. Among the oldest excavated sites in Afghanistan is a temple complex at Sorkh Kowtal, located between Baghlan and Pol-e Khomri in ancient Bactria. It consists of a principal temple and a *cella* (square area marked by four column bases). A secondary temple leans against the exterior wall of the main temple and contains a square fire altar (Zoroastrian). A staircase of monumental proportions reaches from top to bottom of the high hill-temple complex, connecting four distinct terraced embankments. The massive horizontal (waterwheel) water-mills of Afghanistan, often associated with karez, are also remnants of ancient architectural traditions. Also of interest is the pigeon tower. These large, ornate towers attract and house pigeons, the droppings of which are collected and used for fertilizer and in tanning leather.

From its very beginning, perhaps 11,000 years ago, the agricultural systems of Afghanistan have been the most important aspect of the country's society and economy. Elements of the ancient systems are described in the *Geoponika*, a book on agriculture written by ancient Greek and Roman scholars. The agricultural population included sedentary farmers, semisedentary farmers, seminomads, and nomads. These groups were both interdependent and occasionally in conflict. Among the land-tenure systems associated with sedentary farmers were

The ancient Greek kingdom of Bactria, located in present-day northern Afghanistan, was home to the country's oldest city, Bactra, the ruins of which are pictured here. Today known as Balkh, much of the ancient part of the city has been pillaged by locals in search of artifacts they can sell.

those controlled by landlords. In them, agricultural production typically involved five elements: land, water, seed, animal power, and human labor. Whoever contributed one of the elements received one-fifth of the crop. Land and water rights were linked and were owned by the landlord. The landlord would typically provide the seed, draft animals might be contributed by the landlord or villagers, and the villagers provided the labor. Those who actually worked the land would typically receive one-fifth to two-fifths of the crop.

The English word *paradise* came from the Persian word *pairidaeza* used in reference to Persian gardens. It is said that a Persian ruler so admired the royal gardens of the Lydian Empire in Anatolia (present-day Turkey), that he established similar gardens throughout the Achaemenid Empire (including in Afghanistan). The gardens were (and still are in some locations) designed on a grand scale. They typically included combinations of trees, shrubs, and flowers, as well as watercourses and fountains. Created to provide aesthetic pleasure, these gardens had a variety of sweet scents, provided shade during hot summer temperatures, included various fruits and flowers, and served as a habitat to attract birds. The gardens of Kandahar and several other urban centers in Afghanistan were well known in the past.

Despite the sophisticated metallurgy and other crafts associated with the region, Afghanistan, like Iran, is particularly well known for its beautiful hand-woven carpets—a tradition of craftsmanship known for more than 2,500 years. Today, most Afghan carpets are of the Buxoro (Bukhara), or Turkoman type, characterized by parallel rows of geometric figures on a dark red field. Most highly regarded are carpets woven in Faryab Province.

Additional Afghan contributions were made in the areas of philosophy, logic, mathematics, and astronomy. They also made substantial contributions to medicine, music, and mechanics. With the arrival of Islam, the region also became a center of scholastic theology, jurisprudence, poetry, and historical scholarship.

CHAPTER 4

The Age of European Imperialism

During the sixteenth and seventeenth centuries, the Persian Safavids and Indian Mughals (Moghuls) unsuccessfully attempted to control Afghanistan. In 1747, the last great Afghan empire rose under the leadership of Ahmad Shah Durrani of Kandahar. The nineteenth century witnessed tribal conflicts and the intrusion of European imperialism (controlling influence) into the area. Afghanistan became a battleground in the rivalry between Great Britain and czarist Russia for control of Central Asia. Two Anglo-Afghan Wars (1839–1842 and 1878–1880) ended inconclusively. In the first, thousands of the British and their camp followers were killed in a shocking retreat from Kabul. After the second Anglo-Afghan War, the British supported Emir Abdur Rahman Khan's claim to the Afghan throne, and then with the collusion of the Russians in the north, they set out to establish the borders all around their version of the nation of Afghanistan. The present-day borders of Afghanistan were entirely drawn up and plotted by British cartographers (mapmakers) without any real acceptance by Afghans. Afghans' conception of their country was much broader, encompassing extensive lands to the east now in Pakistan and north of the Amu Dar'ya border on the north. Then, with British arms, Abdur Raman, known as the Iron Emir (1880–1901) subdued rebellious Pashtuns, as well as other formerly autonomous tribal groups, and successfully consolidated the Afghan state. He resettled groups of Pashtun families all around the north of the country to exert greater control in regions where Pashtuns had never been very welcome previously. Some observers claim that much of Afghanistan's recent tribal conflict can be traced to Abdur Rahman's policies, which were implemented more than a century ago.

In 1893, Great Britain established an unofficial border, the Durand Line, which separated Afghanistan from British India, and separated ethnically related tribal groups of Pashtuns and other tribal groups as well. The artificial Wakhan Corridor panhandle was also established as a classic narrow buffer zone to keep border problems to a minimum. From a British perspective, Afghanistan was both a buffer between its Indian colony and czarist Russia, and an element of a more ambitious objective—clear global dominance. This objective prompted numerous nineteenth-century exploratory expeditions and was later expressed in British geographer Sir Halford Mackinder's "Heartland Theory." This theory was first expressed in 1904 and was greatly expanded upon in his book *Democratic Ideals and Reality*, published in 1919. Mackinder believed that it was important to control the interior of Eurasia, an area he called the "Heartland," part of the "World Island." His statement, which had a profound impact on political geography and the military policy of many countries, read:

Who rules East Europe commands the Heartland
Who rules the Heartland commands the World
   Island;
Who rules the World Island commands the World.

Similar sentiments were expressed by Lord George Curzon, who was the British Viceroy of India from 1898 to 1905:

Turkistan, Afghanistan, Transcaspia, Persia—to many these words breathe only a sense of utter remoteness or a memory of strange vicissitudes and moribund romance. To me, I confess they are the pieces on a chessboard upon which is being played out a game for the dominance of the World.

Pronouncements such as those made by Mackinder and Curzon clearly help to explain Britain's interest in the region. Once again, Afghanistan was a pawn in someone else's game of power and control.

INDEPENDENCE

Following the third Anglo-Afghan War in 1919, in which the Afghans tried to invade British India and the British used aerial bombers against Kabul for the first time, Afghanistan gained full control over its foreign affairs under the conditions of the Treaty of Rawalpindi. The country thus became fully independent. In 1921, an Afghan-Soviet treaty of friendship was signed, further reducing outside pressures on the country. However, the Soviets needed first to consolidate their new empire's hold on its rebellious regions directly to the north and in other areas before resuming their southward penetration in the Cold War following World War II.

KING AMANULLAH

Emir Amanullah founded an Afghan monarchy in 1926 and undertook a tour of several Middle Eastern and European countries. He returned to Kabul eager to promote European concepts regarding social change and economic development. He decreed that women should go unveiled in Kabul and that men should wear European clothing. He presented his ideas to a *loya jirgeh* (traditional council). Most of the participants were strongly attached to the traditional way of life. They sided with the Muslim religious and tribal leaders strongly opposed to these foreign innovations.

In 1928, the Shinwari Pashtun gained control of Jalalabad, and the Tajik Habibullah Ghazi (better known as Bacheh Saqqo) assembled his followers to the north of Kabul. The forces of Bacheh Saqqo attacked the outskirts of Kabul in December 1928, and in January 1929 Amanullah abdicated in favor of his older brother, Inayatullah, and fled to Kandahar hoping to recruit tribesmen loyal to him and regain the throne. Inayatullah ruled for three days before Bacheh Saqqo entered the capital, proclaimed himself emir, or ruler, and revoked the initiatives of Amanullah. The Soviets, who had supported Amanullah's efforts in modernization, were convinced that the British had backed Bacheh Saqqo and took active steps to restore Amanullah to the throne. However, they were unsuccessful in doing so.

NADIR SHAH

Members of the powerful Musahiban family gathered Pashtun tribal elements and regained control of Kabul in October 1929. Nadir Khan was proclaimed ruler; his coronation as Nadir Shah took place in November. He restored order throughout the country. He also abandoned the emphasis upon rapid modernization, promoted economic development, and was responsible for the drafting of the 1931 constitution—a somewhat conservative version of Amanullah's 1923 constitution. In November 1933, Nadir Shah was assassinated by a supporter of Amanullah, and his eldest son, Muhammad Zahir, succeeded to the throne at 19 years of age.

King Amanullah—pictured here in 1930, shortly after he abdicated the throne to his older brother, Inayatullah—ruled Afghanistan from 1919 to 1929. After helping Afghanistan gain its independence from Great Britain in 1919, Amanullah was responsible for modernizing the country by supporting equal rights and increasing trade with European nations.

MUHAMMAD ZAHIR

Although Muhammad Zahir had become king, the affairs of state were initially in the hands of his uncles, Muhammad Hashim, who served as prime minister from 1933 to 1946, and Sardar Shah Mahmud Kahn, who served as prime minister until 1953—at which time his cousin Sirdar (Prince) Muhammad Daoud Khan became prime minister through a bloodless coup d'état.

Under the leadership of Muhammad Hashim, Afghanistan ended its policy of isolation, foreign trade was expanded, and many schools were constructed. While essentially neutral during World War II, Afghanistan honored the request by the British and Soviets to expel all nationals of the Axis nations (countries supporting Germany and Italy in World War II) who did not enjoy diplomatic status. This decision halted the delivery of equipment and the construction of several new factories being developed with German assistance. In 1946, immediately after the end of World War II, Afghanistan took another major step in becoming more involved in the global community when it joined the United Nations (UN).

In subsequent years, under Shah Mahmud, the Afghans promoted the creation of an independent Pashtunistan. Their goal was to eventually reunite Pashtun tribesmen separated by the Durand Line. They also sought to shift from the encouragement of private enterprise to state control over finance, commerce, and industry. Additionally, they engaged in economic development financed largely by foreign grants and loans and ostensibly maintained a foreign policy of nonalignment (neutrality in conflicts involving other countries). The government of Shah Mahmud also developed the Helmand Valley Authority (HVA) launched by his predecessor. The HVA was an ambitious river-basin development project regulated by high dams on the Helmand and Arghandab rivers. It was a high-level agreement between the United States and Afghanistan that was a focal point of the

THE DECADE OF DAOUD KHAN

The foreign policy of Shah Mahmud had favored the West, rather than maintaining traditional Afghan neutrality. In the early 1950s, frustrated by little progress with regard to the creation of Pashtunistan, increased U.S. aid to Pakistan, and the apparent lack of American interest in Afghan problems, Daoud seized control of the government. Also among Daoud's concerns were issues related to the HVA. The project was designed to permit the cultivation of two grain crops annually. Instead, because of inadequate soil surveys prior to the initiation of the project, progressively increasing salinization, waterlogging, and other problems, crop yields declined by 50 percent, or even more in some areas. Because an engineering firm from the United States had designed the project, the failure affected Afghan trust in American technical assistance.

Daoud's government moved closer to the Soviet Union to restore balance in foreign affairs and to profit from Cold War competition between the two superpowers. As in the past, the Soviets promoted modernization, including state-planned efforts in economic development. Soviet technicians—including petroleum and mining geologists, seismic engineers, veterinarians, agricultural specialists, and others—actively participated in exploration for petroleum and minerals, the construction of factories, the expansion of telephone and telegraph lines, and a variety of agricultural projects. Laws were passed permitting freedom of the press, and various student movements flourished.

The unwillingness of the United States to support construction of a road connecting Afghanistan with the port of Chabahar in Iran on the Arabian Sea further encouraged cooperation with the Soviet Union. The road would have eliminated the necessity of transporting goods through Pakistan, thus separating considerations of trade from the issue of Pashtunistan. It would have permitted access to established markets in India, the Middle East, and Europe, rather than having to create new markets in the Soviet Union. The Soviets responded with commodity-exchange arrangements, such as the exchange of petroleum and building materials for Afghan wool, raw cotton, and hides. A major Soviet loan then resulted in the construction of many facilities. They built two hydroelectric plants and constructed many roads, bridges, and the Salang Tunnel (a two-mile-long [3.2-kilometers-long] tunnel, the world's second highest, through the Hindu Kush range north of Kabul). They also improved port facilities at Shir Khan (on the Amu Dar'ya) and built or upgraded airports, irrigation dams, and canals. The Soviets also improved automotive maintenance and repair facilities and built a materials-testing laboratory and a fertilizer factory. The projects served Soviet self-interest, and the highways and bridges were engineered to support the military traffic that eventually used them. As Nikita Khrushchev noted in his memoirs, *Khrushchev Remembers*:

> There's no doubt that if the Afghans hadn't become our friends, the Americans would have managed to ingratiate themselves with their "humanitarian aid," as they call it. The amount of money we spent in gratuitous assistance to Afghanistan is a drop in the ocean compared to the price we would have had to pay in order to counter the threat of an American military base on Afghan territory.

As usual during the Cold War, increased U.S. aid followed Soviet aid and grew steadily as Daoud exploited competition between the two superpowers.

Soviet inroads into Afghanistan rekindled memories of the efforts of czarist Russia to expand southward to the warm waters of the Arabian Sea and Persian Gulf. To counter these

The Age of European Imperialism

Salang Tunnel, which cuts through the Hindu Kush Mountains, links northern and southern Afghanistan and was completed in 1964. The two-mile-long (3.2-kilometers-long) tunnel was a joint venture with the Soviet Union and was once the highest tunnel in the world, at an elevation of more than 11,000 feet (3,353 meters).

inroads, Americans offered assistance motivated by efforts to contain communism and to develop joint military pacts to halt communist aggression. In its efforts to contain communism, the United States established several treaty organizations that joined together a number of countries that would support U.S. political interests in the region. These alliances included the Southeast Asia Treaty Organization (SEATO), the Central Treaty Organization (CENTO), and the North Atlantic Treaty Organization (NATO).

Nevertheless, the Soviet Union and the United States continued their efforts to gain favor with the Afghans through investment in high-profile assistance projects. When the U.S.-based Export-Import Bank turned down a 1953 Afghan request to pave Kabul's streets, the Soviets assisted in paving some of them. When, in 1956, the Afghans proposed Kandahar as a pivotal center for air traffic in the Middle East-South Asia corridor, the United States constructed the Kandahar International Airport. At about the same time, the Americans suggested that production of high-quality topographic maps of the whole country made from aerial photographs would be essential to development. The Soviets objected to any American flights close to their borders and instead proposed their own flights and mapmaking for the northern quarter of the country. Later in the 1960s, when the two map sets were compared, they did not link together, but whether this was deliberate or due to incompetence was never determined. Some American assistance obviously was extended with genuine concern for the well-being of its recipients. But as was true of Soviet assistance, many of its grants and loans were typically linked to the American need for strong allies, for military bases on foreign soil, or for the control of strategic resources.

The Soviet Union claimed to provide extensive aid to other countries without imposing terms incompatible with their national interests and dignity. They boasted that there were never military or political strings attached to their aid. In reality, however, the Soviets believed that it was unnecessary to attach military and political strings. They thought economic penetration was the easiest and most logical way to influence all institutions in a society. Despite claims of social sensitivity, Soviet policy was devastating to the affected societies in Central Asia. In his book *Afghanistan*, Louis Dupree wrote:

> Generally, the removal of indigenous Muslim religious leaders accelerated forced collectivization or

industrialization. After Russification had taken root and religion had been successfully deemphasized, especially in its ritual [and] symbolic aspects, the Soviets often permitted Communist-sanitized Islam to exist. Communist theorists concluded political Communism can be made compatible with any form of religion through a shift in economic patterns and the removal of religiously oriented vested interest groups.

Soviet efforts in promoting modernization marginalized Afghan traditionalists. It also understandably conflicted with the beliefs of many Afghan religious leaders. These two miscalculations eventually were major factors in leading to the collapse of the Soviet Union. The approach taken by the Soviets is somewhat similar to later U.S. policies involving the expansion of market economies and the forceful removal of the country's ruling Taliban government. The point is not a matter of right or wrong; rather, it is one of a foreign power imposing its will on Afghanistan's people, economy, and government.

The United States and the Soviet Union were not the only countries active in Afghanistan. Diplomatic relations had been established with many countries during the reign of Amanullah. It was within the context of increasingly complex international relationships that the Afghans attempted to understand their relationship with the United States. Dupree wrote:

> The seeming inconsistencies in United States foreign policy, however, puzzled Afghans, as well as many Americans. Some Afghans cannot understand why the United States and the Soviet Union, staunch allies in World War II, became post-war antagonists so quickly. Conversely, the United States alignment with West Germany and Japan, former blood enemies, runs counter to the Afghan concept of loyalty. American policies with regard to Israel, the Arab States, Kashmir, and

"P[a]shtunistan" also baffle the Afghans. Beyond all comprehension were the American frantic efforts to bring neutral nations into military regional pacts.

Despite the Afghans' concern about U.S. loyalties, further attempts were made to secure arms from the United States. However, U.S. policy required that weapons provided by the United States be used only to resist aggression. From an Afghan perspective, it was not clear what was considered to be aggression, or who was to define it. For example, Afghans considered the French to be aggressors in Algeria and political Zionists to be aggressors in Palestine—whereas the French and Americans viewed the relationships quite differently. Further, U.S. airplanes and weapons were used to subdue Pashtun "rebels" in Pakistan. It is often difficult to identify the aggressor in a civil war, a revolution, or an action taken against an unjust regime.

Failing to secure military assistance from the United States, the Afghans obtained small arms, tanks, fighter aircraft, bombers, and helicopters from the Soviet Union, Czechoslovakia, Poland, Hungary, and East Germany. The Soviets also assisted in the construction of military airfields near Mazar-e Sharif, Bagram, and Shindand. At the time, both Washington and Moscow assumed that the provision of military support implied that there was an alliance and, in this case, the U.S. Army believed that Afghanistan had "gone Communist." In fact, the Afghans still regarded themselves as being nonaligned. As Daoud commented:

> Our whole life, our whole existence, revolves around one single focal point—freedom. Should we ever get the feeling that our freedom is in the slightest danger, from whatever quarter, then we should prefer to live on dry bread, or even starve, sooner than accept help that would restrict our freedom.

In the early 1960s, the exclusive competition between the Americans and Soviets in Afghanistan effectively ended. Both countries became actively involved in technical-assistance projects throughout the country, and both provided military training for Afghan officers. While the United States and the Soviet Union both hoped to gain an ally and counter the moves of the other, the Afghans saw little difference between the two. Their relationships with the Soviet Union and the United States tended to reinforce Afghan nationalism, while serving the government's efforts in modernization.

PURDAH AND THE CHADRI

The government of King Amanullah fell in 1929 in part because it abolished purdah and the *chadri* and established coeducational schools in Kabul. Nonetheless, the government of Daoud initiated similar measures in modernization. Purdah is an ancient system in what later became Muslim and Hindu societies of screening women from strangers. The chadri (or burka in other languages) is a sacklike garment of pleated, colored silk or rayon, which covers the entire body from head to toe. An embroidered latticework covers the eyes and permits limited vision. In general, the chadri is used in urban settings by middle-class women (peasant women cannot afford either the cost or the inconvenience of the chadri when working in the fields). Prior to taking these steps toward modernization, the Daoud government carefully examined the Qur'an and Hadith, which is the record of the sayings of Muhammad, and the Hanafi sharia of Sunni Islam, which is a school of Islamic law. It found no mention of a requirement for either purdah or the wearing of a chadri.

It was clear that Islam, as a faith, did not regard women as being inferior to men. Historically, Muslim women have played important roles in social, political, and economic matters. In fact, the customs of purdah and the chadri also were associated with wealthy, urbanized Christian and Zoroastrian women in

In traditional Afghan society, women controlled the inward world of the home and family, whereas men were responsible for interacting with the outside world. Pictured here are Afghan men doing business with roadside vendors in Kabul.

the lands of the Byzantine and Sassanian empires conquered by the Arabs in the seventh century A.D. It appears that purdah and the chadri were adopted by nomadic Arab women in part because doing so conferred the perceived status of the urban women of the civilizations conquered. Many other factors also may have been involved in their adoption, including that the chadri ensured that all women were equal in public places. It is true that the customs entered Afghanistan with the arrival of Islam. Further, as with many cultures, those of the Middle East attach importance to complementary "inward" and "outward" gender relationships. Women control the inward world of the home and family, whereas men are responsible for interaction with the world beyond the home. Adoption of purdah and the chadri helped to reinforce these relationships.

Perhaps the most outspoken opposition to the abolition of purdah and the chadri came from Muslim clerics. They accused the government of abandoning Islam in favor of the values of atheistic communism and the Christian West. They realized that many aspects of urban popular culture, including the cinema, music, and less formal social relationships, were attractive to some people—particularly the young. These foreign influences, they realized, posed a great threat to traditional Afghan culture. Kandahar was, and remains, a center of religious conservatism. As with the later Taliban, resistance to the new policies emerged most dramatically in Kandahar with the riots of 1959.

The issue of Pashtunistan continued to surface, and its creation was strongly supported by the Daoud government. Pakistan, now allied with the United States, strongly opposed the creation of a Pashtunistan. Violence erupted on both sides of the border and, in 1961, Afghan troops advanced across the border. While the Afghans were successful in conventional warfare, they were no match for Pakistan's jet fighter planes. Rather than becoming a full-scale war, the conflict devolved into occasional skirmishes and a continuing war of words.

In Middle Eastern countries—largely creations of European policy or convenience—relationships are typically driven more by ethnicity than by national identity. Indeed, in some instances, divisions *within* ethnic groups can play an important role. For example, Pashtun tribes often fought each other. Sometimes tribes would ally themselves with either Afghanistan or Pakistan in search of greater support and favor. On occasion, all Pashtun tribes would unite in opposition to Pakistan. The somewhat arbitrary creation of countries and their national borders by Europeans simply added a variable that could be included in local political tribal and ethnic strategies. A common technique of the British colonialists, for example, was "divide and rule," whereby national borders were put right through the middle of ethnic groups in order to weaken them and to facilitate manipulative rule by the outsiders.

At the national level, diplomatic relationships were broken between Afghanistan and Pakistan, and the border was closed. Because Afghanistan is landlocked, its exports had traditionally traveled southward through Pakistan to ports on the Arabian Sea. It was assumed by many that Afghanistan would take into account the economic costs of its stance and relent. Typically, however, Afghan pride overrode practical considerations, and it refused to yield. Instead, Afghanistan established even closer economic ties with the Soviet Union to the north, which placed the United States in an awkward position. The United States had allied itself with Pakistan but continued to attach importance to Afghanistan in relation to its strategy of Soviet containment. Pakistan then requested that the United Kingdom represent its interests in Kabul. This proposal was unacceptable to the Afghans. They regarded the British, who had imposed the Durand Line, and who had fought three prior wars directly against them, to be the ultimate culprit in the difficulties that they were experiencing. Further, as one Afghan intellectual cited by Louis Dupree commented, "The British are using America to reassert themselves in Asia. America is still a British colony whether it chooses to believe it or not." This important period in Afghan history came to an end, when, in 1963, Prime Minister Daoud was forced to resign because of the numerous problems the closed border with Pakistan had caused.

THE CONSTITUTIONAL PERIOD

Although Daoud had served the country well as its prime minister, many people were pleased with his resignation. Some hoped that the border with Pakistan would reopen, permitting normal trade relations to the south. Pashtun nomads hoped that they could again follow traditional migratory routes all along the Afghanistan-Pakistan border—routes that had been cut off by closure of the border. Residents of Kabul anticipated a greater availability of consumer goods and reduced prices. Socially conservative Afghans looked forward to a return to traditional values, because Daoud had agreed to all Soviet initiatives in modernization, which they emphatically did not want. They particularly resented initiatives that altered the status of women in society. Civil servants, professionals, and students looked forward to increased emphasis upon social and political reforms that had been neglected during the Pashtunistan crisis. Americans and Germans were pleased, believing that their equipment and commercial goods might soon reach Afghanistan through Pakistan. Iranians hoped to claim some credit for their efforts in promoting better relations between Afghanistan and Pakistan. And Pakistan was pleased with the anticipated reduction of tension along the border and normalized trade.

Other Afghans were uncomfortable with Daoud's resignation—particularly supporters of the concept of Pashtunistan. Members of the royal family were concerned by a possible erosion of their authority in the affairs of government, and many military officers and intellectuals were committed to their country's ongoing relationship with the Soviet Union, in part because they fervently believed in the overinflated values of Communist socialism that were being promoted at the time. Sadly they did not realize how those hollow values could be used to manipulate naïve people for the benefit of foreign interests.

Although Muhammad Zahir Shah officially served as king of Afghanistan from 1933 to 1973, it wasn't until he implemented a constitutional monarchy in 1964 that he fully took control of the country. Zahir Shah (*second from left*) is pictured here at a meeting in Paris with French president Charles de Gualle; de Gualle's wife, Yvonne (*left*); and his wife, Homaira (*right*), in 1963.

With Daoud's departure, Muhammad Zahir Shah firmly grasped the reins of government. Although he had reigned for 30 years, the affairs of government had been in the hands of his uncles and his cousin Daoud, but now he was in control. The king then separated the royal family from the executive branch of government, preparing the way for the formation of a constitutional monarchy. Daoud was replaced as prime minister by Muhammad Yousuf, who had served as Minister of Mines and Industries. Policies under Yousuf differed little from those of his predecessor. There was, however, a somewhat greater emphasis on private enterprise, the need for constitutional reform, and efforts to establish a more representative system of government.

Several measures first initiated by Daoud's government came to pass: The value of Afghan currency was stabilized with support from the International Monetary Fund; the Soviet Union and the United States agreed to undertake new road projects; Ariana Afghan Airlines purchased new aircraft in the United States and expanded its services; the U.S. Peace Corps became actively involved in Afghanistan; and the United States committed the funds necessary to complete the construction of Kabul University. Freedom of the press was also expanded, and prison reforms were initiated. In the past, Afghan prisons had emphasized punishment rather than rehabilitation, and prisoners were often shackled and beaten, or in the nineteenth century even starved to death. In May 1963, the Iranian government invited Afghan and Pakistani delegations to Tehran. It successfully negotiated the restoration of diplomatic and trade relations between the two former enemies. Finally, the most important accomplishment of the government was the introduction of a new constitution in 1964. The constitution was believed by many to be the finest in the Muslim world. With its acceptance, Afghanistan became a hereditary constitutional monarchy.

Despite a continuing U.S. presence in Afghanistan during the 1960s, the energies of the United States were increasingly diverted by its involvement in the Vietnam War. As Joseph Collins wrote in *The Soviet Invasion of Afghanistan* (1986):

> [During this period] Soviet economic aid continued along with Soviet developmental assistance, in spite of its aggregate decrease in value during the Vietnam War, hitting 70 percent of total Afghan aid during the period 1967–70. This was in marked contrast to the United States whose aid during this period dipped temporarily from one-third of total Afghan aid in

1967 to less than 3 percent of the total in 1969. By 1973, total Soviet military and economic aid ($1.5 billion) outweighed U.S. economic aid ($425 million) by a factor of three to one.

Although by 1967 the Afghan armed forces had become almost wholly dependent upon the Soviets, Afghans were often critical of Soviet policy and attempted to maintain their nonaligned status.

While the 1964 constitution addressed a broad range of important issues, its promotion of modernization offended many traditionalists. Further, the king discouraged the long-term development of political parties, and the separation of powers within the government was extreme. The prime minister was responsible to the king, but had little influence over Parliament. The king himself exercised little leadership, hoping that the system would function effectively of its own accord. Finally, members of the royal family were no longer permitted to participate in political parties or to hold the following offices: prime minister or minister, member of Parliament, or justice of the Supreme Court. Because the day-to-day operation of the government had been in the hands of the royal family for decades, governance fell into less-experienced hands. Daoud and other individuals who could have contributed became disaffected. Further, the pace of social change was disorienting to many people. Urban growth was accompanied by accelerated modernization. Expanded educational opportunity resulted in a dramatic increase in high school and university graduates, but employment opportunities were limited. Finally, the country had no planning program, a poorly developed banking system, and no civil service.

There was rapid turnover within the government. Student protests erupted, and their often-violent suppression alienated many students. In an October 1965 demonstration, Afghan troops fired upon student protesters, leaving three dead and several wounded. Student-worker protests occurred in 1968. Policemen quelling a demonstration in the spring of 1969 killed several students, and student protests once again erupted in 1971. The initial protests were largely nonideological. Increasingly, however, both alienated politicians and frustrated students sought solutions by more radical political means.

The People's Democratic Party of Afghanistan (PDPA), led by Nur Muhammad Taraki and Babrak Karmal, became a vehicle for opposition to the government. Taraki was a well-known liberal intellectual who had been a government bureaucrat and a translator for the American diplomatic mission. Karmal had served in the government and had twice been elected to Parliament. The party sought to establish a socialist society that adapted Marxist-Leninist principles to conditions in Afghanistan.

THE RETURN OF DAOUD KHAN

The results of the elections of 1969 revealed that Afghan tribal leaders, who were both socially and religiously conservative, had developed a better understanding of the electoral process. In the election, they gained control of Parliament. They did so with the goal of preserving traditional values and limiting further efforts in modernization. Following his departure from Afghan politics in 1963, Daoud had conducted an ongoing discussion with army officers and political activists. By this dialogue, he hoped to assess the strengths and weaknesses of his regime (1953–1963) and what might be done to solve the problems of contemporary Afghanistan. Dissatisfied with the direction taken in Afghan politics since his departure, Daoud, with support from the army and the palace guard, overthrew the monarchy in 1973. Muhammad Zahir Shah, at the time vacationing in Italy, was exiled. His family later joined him.

Daoud immediately made many changes in the way the country was governed. He established a military government and reaffirmed his commitment to basic Islamic principles.

Additionally, his policy of nonalignment was reconstituted, and he promised to seek a peaceful resolution of the Pashtunistan issue. Among other actions, Daoud strengthened the army and the institutions of government and further expanded Afghanistan's relationship with the Soviet Union. He also attempted to develop an industrial sector that would replace agriculture and handicrafts as the principal sources of wealth in the country. Through industrialization, Daoud hoped to generate a broad base of popular support within Afghanistan. He hoped to eventually lead the country into greater political and economic independence. If this was to be accomplished, he had to have the means to more aggressively pursue future efforts toward modernization. To achieve these ends, he introduced a new constitution in 1977 that banned all political parties other than his own—the National Revolutionary Party. The Republic of Afghanistan was then formally established; Daoud was proclaimed president. He also assumed responsibility for defense and foreign affairs.

Resistance to Daoud's policies surfaced almost immediately. Some Kabul-based groups believed that the pace of modernization was too deliberate. More conservative groups in rural areas felt that modernization should be abandoned altogether. It was at this time that militant tribal leaders, the mujahideen, entered Afghan politics. Armed and trained by Pakistan, a number of mujahideen leaders attacked politically sensitive targets in an effort to undermine the Daoud government. Many urban political activists who were supported by the Soviets represented an even greater threat to Daoud, who attempted to purge these elements from both the military and government. In response, many of the same elements of the army that had brought him to power in 1973 overthrew him in a bloody military coup in 1978. In this so-called Saur Revolution, Daoud, his family, and the presidential guard were all killed. This event ushered in still another era in Afghanistan's turbulent political history.

# Chapter 5

The Soviet Invasion and Its Aftermath

With the death of Daoud, Nur Muhammad Taraki, the leader of the Khalq ("Masses") faction of the PDPA, assumed the presidency. Almost immediately, conflict arose between the Khalq and the more moderate Parcham ("Flag") faction. Further, there was growing resistance in rural communities to the communists' modernization initiatives. Among the initiatives were land reform, industrialization, and literacy programs, some of which would have benefited rural populations. Hence, while the communist factions were engaged in their own struggle, mullahs and khans (religious and tribal leaders) declared a jihad (holy war) against the communist infidels (non-Muslims). President Taraki was assassinated in 1979, and his Khalq successor, Hafizullah Amin, was killed when 85,000 Soviet troops were dispatched to Kabul in December 1979. Ironically, the troops had been requested by President

Amin. But the Soviets felt that the civil strife created by Khalq policies threatened their influence and investments in Afghanistan, as well as the security of the Soviet republics to the north. They therefore deposed Amin and his supporters and replaced them with Babrak Karmal of the Parcham faction, and his more moderate approach to socialist reform.

THE SOVIET UNION INVADES AFGHANISTAN

With the 1979 Soviet invasion, Afghanistan found itself in the midst of an intensified competition between the Soviet Union and the United States. The conservative mujahideen were the chief opponents of the Soviets and their Afghan allies. The jihad gained momentum as the United States, China, and Arab states provided the mujahideen with money, arms, other supplies, and logistical support to partially offset the equivalent of approximately U.S. $45 billion invested by the Soviets in their unsuccessful effort to defeat the mujahideen. The United States committed roughly $5 billion, a sum matched by Saudi Arabia and other contributors. Most of the aid was in the form of modern weapons, including U.S. Stinger missiles. The Ghilzai Pashtun, concentrated in eastern Afghanistan and around the capital city of Kabul, were the chief recipients of aid directed to the mujahideen. The Durrani Pashtun, located in southern Afghanistan and the Kandahar region, received comparatively little support.

In 1986, Babrak Karmal resigned as president and was replaced by an associate, Muhammad Najibullah. In 1988, the leaders of several Afghan factions formed an interim government in exile based in Pakistan. The Soviet government faced broadening Islamic opposition, soaring economic costs to support the Afghanistan conflict (including the average loss of a helicopter a day to the Stinger missiles), and the political costs of the conflict at home and abroad. The Soviets finally withdrew the last of their troops in 1989. For most Afghans, the Soviet invasion had simply been another attempt by foreigners

In 1979, the Soviet Union invaded Afghanistan in order to defeat the mujahideen, insurgents who were trying to overthrow the Marxist government. The Soviet-Afghan War lasted 10 years and resulted in more than 1.5 million Afghan deaths, but the mujahideen were ultimately successful in driving the Soviets from Afghanistan. This statue of a Soviet tank, in Herat, is dedicated to the Afghan people, who nobly defended their country during the conflict.

to dominate them. The Soviets, as had so many others, had tried to replace Afghan Islamic beliefs and other cultural traditions with an alien ideology and social system.

At a cost of more than 1.5 million Afghan lives—roughly equal to the combined populations of Montana and North Dakota—the mujahideen and their "Arab Afghan" allies had contributed to one of the most significant events of the twentieth century. They played what some observers believe to have been a major role in bringing about the collapse of the Soviet Union and with it, the retreat of international Communism. Among the so-called "Arab Afghan" fighters, however, very few were Afghans and relatively few were Arabs. They were composed of volunteers from nearly 60 different countries.

THE WAR'S AFTERMATH

The International Committee of the Red Cross noted that the conflict with the Soviets and its aftermath left 98,000 Afghan families headed by widows and 63,000 headed by disabled people. The conflict and its aftermath also left 500,000 disabled orphans. Many children, as well as adults, were killed or crippled by land mines laid during the 1979–1989 conflict. This problem was compounded during the 2001–2002 military conflict by the presence of unexploded bombs—particularly cluster bombs. These weapons were attractive to children and could also easily be mistaken for the yellow food packages that had been dropped from U.S. aircraft.

Owing in part to the destruction of wells, karez, and storage and distribution systems, today only 12 percent of the population has access to clean drinking water. For the past decade, Afghanistan has suffered the world's highest infant mortality rate. The lack of pure water supplies is a major factor contributing to the death of one out of every four children before the age of five. Afghanistan's rate for death of women in childbirth is also the highest in the world. Additionally, the conflict destroyed 12,000 of the country's 22,000 villages and some 2,000 schools. More than 6 million Afghans sought shelter in Pakistan and Iran, and many remained as refugees during the turbulent years following the Soviet withdrawal. The number of Afghan refugees in Pakistan alone rose from an estimated 18,000 in 1978 to 2.8 million in 1982.

Armed opposition to the regime of President Najibullah followed the Soviet withdrawal in 1988–1989. Najibullah was overthrown in 1992, and the mujahideen captured Kabul. Much of the subsequent conflict occurred as a result of the fact that Kabul did not fall to the well-armed Pashtun factions based in Peshawar. Rather, it fell to the Tajik forces of

Burhanuddin Rabbani and his military commander Ahmad Shah Masoud, and to the Uzbek forces of Rashid Dostum. It was the first time in 300 years that Pashtuns had lost control of Kabul, and Gulbuddin Hekmatyar rallied Pashtun forces in an attempt to reclaim the city.

Afghanistan itself was virtually fragmented. The country was essentially divided into fiefdoms—small warring states in which factions fought, switched sides, and fought again in a bewildering array of alliances, betrayals, and bloodshed. The largely Tajik government of Rabbani controlled Kabul and northeastern Afghanistan. Dostum, an Uzbek leader and former communist sympathizer, controlled the several northern provinces. The eastern border provinces were controlled by a council of mujahideen commanders based in Jalalabad. A small region to the southeast of Kabul was under the control of Hekmetyar. In central Afghanistan, the Hazaras controlled the province of Bamiyan. Much of western Afghanistan was controlled from Herat by Ismael Khan. Southern Afghanistan was divided among several minor mujahideen leaders and bandits who plundered the population at will. According to Ahmed Rashid in his book *Taliban*:

> International aid agencies were fearful of even working in Kandahar as the city itself was divided by warring groups. Their leaders sold off everything to Pakistani traders to make money, stripping down telephone wires and poles, cutting trees, selling off factories, machinery and even road rollers to scrap merchants. The warlords seized homes and farms, threw out their occupants and handed them over to their supporters. The commanders abused the population at will, kidnapping young girls and boys for their sexual pleasure, robbing merchants in the bazaars and fighting and brawling in the streets. Instead of refugees returning from Pakistan, a fresh wave of refugees began to leave Kandahar for Quetta.

In 1994, Dostum abandoned his alliance with the Rabbani government and joined with Hekmetyar to attack Kabul. The following conflict led to a second generation of mujahideen, the Taliban. Because most of those involved in the formation of the Taliban were students at madrassas, the name was easily acquired. A *talib* is an Islamic student, or one who seeks knowledge, as opposed to a mullah, or one who imparts knowledge. A madrassa is a school in which the Qur'an and the practices of Islam are mainly taught, but the term may also be applied to any school for students up to age 17 or 18.

RISE AND FALL OF THE TALIBAN

Mullah Muhammad Hassan, the governor of Kandahar, described some of the reasons for the formation of the Taliban:

> We all knew each other—Mullahs Omar, Ghaus, Mohammed Rabbani (no relation to President Rabbani) and myself—because we were all originally from Urozgan province and had fought together. I moved back and forth from Quetta and attended madrassas there, but whenever we got together we would discuss the terrible plight of our people living under these bandits. We were people of the same opinions and we got on with each other very well, so it was easy to come to a decision to do something.

Taliban leaders were largely battle-hardened Pashtuns with strong support from the government of Pakistan. Mullah Muhammad Omar lost his right eye in 1989, when a rocket exploded nearby; Mullah Hassan lost a leg in the war; former justice minister Nuruddin Turabi and former foreign minister Muhammad Ghaus are also one-eyed; the former Taliban mayor of Kabul, Abdul Majid, is missing one leg and two fingers; and other leaders suffer similar disabilities. The wounds were a constant reminder of the 20 years of warfare that had devastated Afghanistan. After much discussion, they agreed upon an agenda: restore peace, disarm the population, defend the integrity and Islamic character of Afghanistan, and enforce sharia (Islamic) law.

Unfortunately, many of the objectives and cultural underpinnings of the Taliban were misunderstood, particularly in the United States. Afghanistan is often said to possess a "warrior society." Its people have long fought to resist external control, but they also have a long tradition of fighting among themselves. While the Taliban were relatively successful in restoring order, they did not hesitate to resort to violence to achieve their objectives. What is often absent in the analysis of such violence is an understanding of the depth of anti-communist sentiment among the Taliban. Also, it is important to recognize the chaotic and violent nature of Afghan society following the war with the Soviets and the limited control exercised by the mullahs over those who share their beliefs.

Similarly, punishment for crimes such as murder or adultery was often severe and conducted in public under the Taliban (although no more so than in many other countries governed by the sharia). It might also be noted that the Taliban's strict interpretation of Islamic law often resulted in punishments that might be viewed as excessively lenient in non-Islamic countries. For example, in the case of murder, Taliban judges encouraged the families of the victim to accept the payment of *diya*, or blood money, rather than put the killer to death. The purpose was to reduce or eliminate the practice of blood feuds that would result in further violence. As Islamic law was already embedded in Afghan culture, its strict enforcement met with widespread public approval and a sharp reduction in crime.

The treatment of women espoused by the Taliban was also widely criticized, particularly the requirement that women wear the chadri when in public. As in other regions of the Islamic world, Muslim women often view the requirement

The Taliban, a Sunni Islamist movement, is known for its strict interpretation of Islamic law and advocates severe and public punishment for crimes such as murder and adultery. Here, Taliban members read from Muslim holy books during their campaign to take the northern Afghan city of Mazar-i Sharif in 1997.

quite differently than women in non-Islamic societies do. For example, as Americans Nancy and Louis Dupree observed:

> Women in the cities [of Afghanistan] continue to come out of purdah (*pardah*) and remove the veil, but a strange reversal of attitudes has occurred in villages becoming towns, brought about by the massive shifts of the transport and communication networks in the 1960s. Village and nomadic women seldom wore the chadri in the past because it would have interfered with their many daily economic functions. Now, however, if

a village grows to town status, complete with a bazaar, and a man gains enough wealth to hire servants, his wife often insists on wearing a chadri, for she believes the custom to be sophisticated and citified—not realizing her city cousins have opposite attitudes. In addition, many young girls in the cities and towns wear the chadri briefly after puberty to indicate they have become bona fide women, ready for marriage.

Further, as noted by Sonia Shah in *The Progressive* (a journal that advocates peace and human rights):

Messy reality sometimes confounds [the] captivating idea that the veil victimizes all the women who wear it. A remarkable but underreported Physicians for Human Rights 2000 survey of 200,000 women and men in Afghanistan, for instance, found that more than three-quarters of women in Afghanistan choose to wear the *chadri* with or without the Taliban's edicts, and 90 percent of respondents thought that the Taliban's clothing edicts were an unimportant issue.

Like issues of criminal justice, conflicting views of the role of the chadri in Afghan society were related less to Taliban edicts than to the differing values of rural and urban Afghanistan and the folk and Westernized cultures associated with them. In Afghanistan, the former vastly outnumber the latter. But Westernized Afghans, including the Revolutionary Association of the Women of Afghanistan, enjoyed greater access to the Western media and were strongly supported by American groups concerned by reports of wanton violence and the oppression of women. In fact, for many Westernized Afghan women, the Taliban edicts dramatically altered their lives. The following edict relating to women, in its original translation from Dari, was issued after the capture of Kabul in 1996:

Women you should not step outside your residence. If you go outside the house you should not be like women who used to go with fashionable clothes wearing much cosmetics and appearing in front of every man before the coming of Islam.

Islam ... as a religion has determined specific dignity for women. Islam has valuable instructions for women. Women should not create such opportunity to attract the attention of useless people who will not look at them with a good eye. Women have the responsibility as a teacher or coordinator for her family. Husband, brother, father have the responsibility for providing the family with the necessary life requirements (food, clothes, etc.). In case women are required to go outside the residence for the purposes of education, social needs or social services they should cover themselves in accordance with Islamic sharia regulation. If women are going outside with fashionable, ornamental, tight and charming clothes to show themselves, they will be cursed by the Islamic sharia and should never expect to go to heaven.

All family elders and every Muslim have responsibility in this respect. We request all family elders to keep tight control over their families and avoid these social problems. Otherwise these women will be threatened, investigated and severely punished as well as the family elders by the forces of the Religious Police (*Munkrat*).

The Religious Police (Munkrat) have the responsibility and duty to struggle against these social problems and will continue their effort until "evil" is finished. There were many other edicts: idolatry (worship of objects rather than God), sorcery, gambling, and the use of addictive substances are unacceptable; female patients should be treated by female physicians; male tailors cannot take measurements of female customers;

men should wear beards, but avoid wearing their hair long (in "British and American hairstyles"); music should not be broadcast in public places; music and dancing are to be avoided at weddings; one should avoid playing drums; keeping birds as a hobby must cease; kite flying should be prevented; interest should not be paid for loans; husbands should be punished if their wives wash clothes in the channels along city streets; and prayer should be performed as required.

The Taliban strongly opposed efforts in modernization that eroded Afghanistan's cultural integrity. Many of the efforts toward modernization were associated with atheistic communism. They similarly resented the erosion of moral values as reflected in Hollywood and Indian films, as well as in television serials. The Taliban thought that the films and serials both degraded women and promoted violence. As Donald Wilber observed 40 years ago in his book *Afghanistan*:

> Westernized Afghans ... are impatient because they believe that Afghanistan must make extremely rapid economic progress if it is to draw abreast of the modern world, and that the ultimate responsibility for such progress falls upon them. The mass of the people like to keep the good old ways, with a profitable change now and then, and here and there, which does not upset the basic structure. Some, among the more influential of the clergy, would even like to go back to the earlier and "purer" ways.

The same could be said today. In many ways, Islamic fundamentalists such as the Taliban are similar to the European Protestants of the sixteenth century. Like the Protestants, Islamic fundamentalists are a relatively new and innovative presence. As political scientist Samuel P. Huntington noted, both modern Islamic fundamentalism and European Protestantism are reactions to the stagnation and corruption of

During its reign, the Taliban opposed any form of modernization that it believed would erode Afghanistan's cultural integrity. For example, women were supposed to cover their faces in public places, which is depicted in this photo taken outside the Blue Mosque in Mazar-i Sharif.

existing institutions. Both advocate a return to a purer and more demanding form of their religion, and both preach work, order, and discipline. In *The Progressive*, Barbara Ehrenreich describes other similarities:

> In sixteenth-century Swiss cantons and seventeenth-century Massachusetts, Calvinists and Calvinist-leaning Protestants banned dancing, gambling, drinking, colorful clothing, and sports of all kinds. They outlawed idleness and vigorously suppressed sexual activity in all but its married, reproductively oriented, form.

Transported back into a Calvinist-run Zurich or Salem, a member of the Taliban might have found only one thing that was objectionable: the presence of unveiled women. But he would have been reassured on this point by the Calvinists' insistence on women's subjugation. As a man is to Jesus, asserted the new Christian doctrine, so is his wife to him.

As previously noted, throughout history Afghans have resisted rapid social change—particularly imposed change that is both socially disorienting and adversely affects the traditional Afghan way of life, including the means of livelihood. Further, while the Afghan fundamentalists are perhaps a "new and innovative presence," they are oriented by past, rather than by future, expectations. Almost any "modern" action is justified on the basis of history. An Afghan who starts to analyze or explain a problem will begin by considering its historical aspects.

With regard to governance, many Muslims prefer a theocratic state, such as the sharia offers. It provides strict standards by which a leader can be judged. Should a leader prove to be unjust, citizens have a right to install new leadership. The attitudes of many Afghans and other Middle Easterners are strongly influenced by a regional history of colonialism, imposed leadership, unresponsive monarchies, and secular dictatorships. Further, Islam provides a coherent alternative framework for the integration of social, economic, and political activity.

Ultimately, the Taliban efforts at social and political reform failed. The fall of the Taliban was variously a consequence of U.S. political and economic interests, gender issues, al Qaeda's presence in Afghanistan, and an unwillingness to compromise.

PETROLEUM POLITICS

After the 1991 collapse of the Soviet Union, Central Asia's vast gas and oil reserves acquired considerable strategic importance for the United States, as well as for American energy companies. Further, as Ahmed Rashid observed, "US oil companies, who had spearheaded the first US forays into the region, now wanted a greater say in US policy-making." American interests realized that control of Central Asian energy resources would reduce American reliance on the resources of the Organization of Petroleum Exporting Countries (OPEC). Such control would help avoid petroleum embargoes such as those of the 1970s that posed a threat to industrialized economies. As Sheila Heslin of the National Security Council noted, it was "U.S. policy to promote the rapid development of Caspian energy ... specifically to promote ... Western energy security through diversification of supply."

The area surrounding the Caspian Sea basin ranks among the world leaders in petroleum reserves. But the crude oil, once tapped, must be transported in some way to secure refining and storage facilities before going to commercial markets. The least expensive and safest way to transport the crude oil is by pipeline. Many pipeline routes have been proposed, and these routes, themselves, have become a major political issue. As former Russian president Boris Yeltsin commented, "We cannot help seeing the uproar stirred up in some Western countries over the energy resources of the Caspian. Some seek to exclude Russia from the game and undermine its interests. The so-called pipeline war in the region is part of this game."

For a number of reasons, both strategic and economic, the proposed Afghanistan routes were favored by U.S. policy makers and energy companies. Chronic political instability in countries through which other routes would pass on their way to the Mediterranean Sea posed problems. Further, the U.S. intelligence community had concluded that with German reunification, the European Union had become a major competitor. Americans reasoned that it would not be in their long-term national interest for Central Asian gas and oil to pass through the (European-controlled) Mediterranean en route to the United States.

The western, or Mediterranean, routes were also longer and correspondingly more difficult to control. The most direct Turkmenistan–Mediterranean route was 1,875 miles (3,017 kilometers) in length; but the most direct route from Turkmenistan to the Arabian Sea, passing through Afghanistan, was only 750 miles (1,207 kilometers) in length. Finally, U.S. energy companies were also intent upon developing Afghanistan pipelines to serve the growing needs of southern and eastern Asia.

In their efforts to establish a trans-Afghanistan pipeline, U.S. energy companies found themselves in competition with Bridas, an Argentinean energy company. Bridas had initiated a feasibility study of an Afghanistan pipeline in March 1995. The following month, the United States set up a working group that included many government agencies and energy companies. Its task was to coordinate U.S. efforts in the exploitation of Central Asia's gas and oil reserves.

When the Taliban gained control of Kabul in September 1996, U.S. governmental officials and the petroleum industry strongly supported them. It was believed that the Taliban were capable of stabilizing the country and establishing a government that could be recognized by the United States. Negotiations regarding the proposed pipeline resulted in Taliban delegations visiting the United States, as well as visits by U.S. officials to Kabul and Kandahar. One U.S. company, Unocal, seeking favor for its desire to develop the region's oil resources, donated $900,000 to the Center for Afghanistan Studies at the University of Nebraska, Omaha. The center, in turn, established a training and humanitarian aid program for Afghans. It opened a school at Kandahar to train teachers, electricians, carpenters, and pipe fitters who could assist with the construction of the proposed pipeline. Along with various gifts given to the Taliban and other expenses, the company estimated that it spent $15 to $20 million on the project.

The Argentine company Bridas also courted the Taliban during this period, and their approach was quite different from that of Unocal. The Argentine company executives expressed interest in Islam, as well as the politics, culture, and history of Afghanistan and the Afghans. They also took the trouble to learn the ethnic, tribal, and family linkages of the leaders with whom they met. By contrast, the U.S. company gathered information from the American Embassy in Islamabad and from Pakistani and Turkmen intelligence agencies. It attempted to achieve its objectives through the application of political and economic pressure. Further, its representatives had little apparent knowledge of, or interest in, Afghanistan. "While Bridas engineers would spend hours sipping tea with Afghan tribesmen in the desert as they explored routes," representatives of the U.S. company would "fly in and out and take for granted what they were told by the notoriously fickle Afghan warlords." The U.S. firm was also at a disadvantage because its policy toward the Taliban did not deviate from the U.S. position; rather, its representatives regularly told the Taliban what they should be doing.

Bridas was ready to sign a deal with the Taliban, even though they were not recognized as the legitimate government by any state. The Taliban did, however, enjoy limited diplomatic recognition, chiefly by conservative states in the Persian Gulf. Taliban support gravitated toward Bridas. In December 1998, the U.S. firm withdrew from the Afghanistan pipeline project consortium, citing low oil prices, concerns about Osama bin Laden being in Afghanistan, and pressure from U.S. feminist groups. The Taliban leaders were quite aware of the potential political and economic costs of their decision.

In the United States, the Taliban had lost political support of both Republicans and Democrats early on, thus greatly increasing their political isolation and vulnerability. Further, both American political parties were able to support the military offensive that would promote American strategic objectives. The presence of Osama bin Laden and al Qaeda in Afghanistan provided policy makers with further justification for a military offensive. Plans for such an offensive began to unfold in 1999 and intensified during the early months of 2001.

OSAMA BIN LADEN AND AL QAEDA

During the war with the Soviet Union in the 1980s, the mujahideen resistance was aided by gifts of money, weapons, and foreign fighters from many countries. Osama bin Laden, wealthy son of a building contractor close to the Saudi Arabian royal family, came to aid in the struggle. After the Soviets were defeated and left Afghanistan in 1988–1989, huge quantities of weapons were left behind by the Soviet Union, as well as by the United States and its Pakistani allies. These weapons enabled Afghanistan to lapse into civil war and ultimately led to the rise of the Taliban. Into this vacuum of power and political chaos, in what was by then referred to as the "failed state" of Afghanistan, bin Laden was able to establish al Qaeda, his network of Islamic terrorists. Camps were established in Afghanistan to train young men in guerrilla warfare and terror tactics that could be exported to the rest of the world. The first truck bombing of the World Trade Center towers in New York City occurred in 1993, followed by the bombing of the American embassies in Kenya and Tanzania in 1998, and the USS *Cole* in the Yemeni port of Aden in 2000. These atrocities and many others were traced back to bin Laden's operatives from his training camps in Afghanistan. Cruise missiles were launched by order of President Clinton against some of these camps in 1998, and other attempts were made with satellites to track down bin Laden and perhaps kill him. In spite of requests from the U.S. government, the Taliban regime in Kabul refused to turn over bin Laden to the United States for trial, and the terrorism training continued. In Afghanistan on September 9, 2001, pro-Taliban suicide bombers assassinated Ahmad Shah Masoud, the leader of the Northern Alliance of Tajik and Uzbek, and others who opposed the Taliban regime. Then two days later, on September 11, 2001, came the passenger airplane attack by bin Laden's Arab operatives on both towers of the World Trade Center in New York City and the Pentagon in Washington, D.C.

OPERATION ENDURING FREEDOM

Shortly after the 9/11 tragedy in which thousands of innocent people lost their lives, the U.S. military coalition launched Operation Enduring Freedom in Afghanistan. The objectives were to destroy bin Laden's terrorist training camps, interrupt the al Qaeda network, and unseat the Taliban government. Bombing began on October 7, 2001, and U.S. Special Forces began the ground combat phase of the operation 12 days later in Kandahar. The Northern Alliance, bolstered by aerial and ground support from the U.S. military coalition, continued its frontline offensive north of Kabul, taking the city on November 13. By late November, U.S. Marines invaded the last remaining Taliban stronghold of Kandahar, and on December 10, the Taliban surrendered there. But bin Laden had not yet been captured and al Qaeda was far from defeated, although its networks were disrupted.

The search for bin Laden and his henchmen was multifaceted, with information coming in from many quarters. Particularly interesting was the role played by physical geography and geology. Immediately after the September 11, 2001, atrocities, a bin Laden tape was broadcast by the Arab television news channel Al Jazeera. Rocks and landforms appearing behind bin Laden could be identified by people familiar with the area of the eastern Spin Ghar (Safed Koh or White Mountains) close to the border with Pakistan. This led to the U.S. military campaign to capture Tora Bora, an area of only several dozen square miles. But Tora Bora is a fortress of snowcapped peaks, steep valleys, and fortified caves and bunkers, and it has many tunnels and bases built some 20 years earlier, during the C.I.A.-financed jihad of the 1980s against the Soviet occupation.

In late November 2001, a small force of about three dozen U.S. troops, joined by a motley contingent of about 2,500 poorly trained, ill-equipped, and easily bribed Northern Alliance forces, faced down 1,500 to 2,000 well-trained, well-armed, and totally committed al Qaeda defenders of Osama bin Laden. In spite of massive and devastating explosions from "bunker buster" and "daisy cutter" bombs, by early December the al Qaeda fighters were still holding on at Tora Bora. On December 12, one of the ineffective Northern Alliance commanders offered a cease-fire, in spite of furious U.S. opposition. During the lull in fighting, on or about December 16, bin Laden left Tora Bora on horseback and on foot and crossed the border to Pakistan through the Parachinar region south of the Spin Ghar Mountains. Over the next few years, bin Laden moved south into Waziristan and then back north into Mohmand and Bajaur in Pakistan, hidden effectively in the lawless and little-tracked Northwest Frontier Province. Here, government allies of the United States are unwelcome, easy to identify by their lack of skill with language and subtle cultural differences, with the result that to date, bin Laden has been able to evade capture.

THE TALIBAN VIEWPOINT

Present-day Muslim political philosophers see existing political boundaries in Southwest Asia as being relics of the colonial past. Today, many of them speak out boldly against the values and institutions introduced by the West. Increasingly, these leaders pose a serious threat to many Middle Eastern governments, Westernized Middle Easterners, and Western governments (including those dependent upon the energy resources of the Middle East). While their objectives and approaches vary, many, including Osama bin Laden, direct their energies toward regional unification. They seek to restore a vast region in which the community of Muslims would be united under a single flag. Their vision is bolstered by what many view as the Golden Age of Islam. During this period that spanned the seventh to

U.S. soldiers of the Fort Campbell-based 1-75 Cavalry fire mortars at a nearby Taliban position at Forward Operating Base Wilson in Kandahar Province, Southern Afghanistan, in 2010.

ninth centuries A.D., Muslim Arab caliphates extended from the Atlantic Ocean into the heart of Central Asia.

Some believe that this hoped-for transformation should be done on a country-by-country basis. Ayatollah Khomeini, for example, transformed Iran from an essentially secular monarchy into an Islamic republic in 1979. Today, many others are searching for mechanisms by which a politically fragmented Middle East can be more quickly transformed into a single Muslim state.

Leaders of this general movement tend to be well educated, wealthy, distinguished in battle, and relatively patient. Their most immediate concern is the long-standing conflict between Israel and the Palestinians. Other important issues include the removal of U.S. troops from Saudi Arabia and the U.S. invasion of Iraq. These and other concerns provide the fuel for al Qaeda fighters to continue the fray against the hated Americans. All these issues pose major challenges to American influence in the Middle East. While the Palestinian issue is complicated, most Middle Easterners, regardless of religion, view the creation of Israel as a European solution to a European problem at their expense and without consultation or consent. In their view, Israel continues to reside in the region as an antagonistic European enclave fully supported by the United States.

The Iraqi invasion of Kuwait was also widely condemned in the Middle East. Bin Laden sought to form a Muslim defense force, including battle-hardened "Arab Afghans," to protect Saudi Arabia. Instead, over the objections of Saudi Arabia's senior religious leaders and some members of the royal family, King Fahd permitted U.S. forces to use Saudi Arabia as a base. The United States promised that its troops would not stay in the country "a minute longer than they were needed." More than a decade later, however, some 20,000 U.S. troops remained based in "the country of the Two Holy Places [Mecca and Medina]." While the Iraqi invasion of Kuwait was condemned, even Iraq's staunchest opponents in the region, Iran and Kuwait, objected to the United Nations sanctions that followed the conflict.

Ominous clouds of dissent hung over Southwest Asia well before the 2001 U.S. military action against Afghanistan, which was triggered by the tragic events of September 11. In 2010, armed conflict continued in Afghanistan, even though the Taliban government and its leadership were eliminated. Their removal opened yet another new and uncertain chapter of Afghan history that has yet to play out in its entirety. Achieving lasting stability and peace in Afghanistan remains an elusive and perhaps distant goal, but many are certainly trying.

In America's second longest war after the Cold War with the Soviet Union, the struggle since 9/11 by the United States and its NATO and other allies in Afghanistan continues against very long odds of success. No one since Alexander the Great more than 2,300 years ago has ever succeeded for long in invading Afghanistan. The Afghan people are well known for allowing the invaders of antiquity to come easily into the country, but getting out unscathed is an altogether different story. The only real way to succeed in taking over Afghanistan is to establish a generous program of development without chaos and corruption. Otherwise, no matter how many battles the invader succeeds in winning, the overall war will still be lost.

Soon after the 9/11 tragedy, the Bush administration was ideologically opposed to nation building in Afghanistan. The invasion of Afghanistan had been done with almost no thought as to the future of the country, and the civilian side was left largely to the United Nations and various volunteer nongovernmental organizations (NGOs). Then to compound the errors, the Bush presidency decided to invade Iraq shortly after the rout of the Taliban by modern weaponry in 2001. This directly competed with the need to maintain security in Afghanistan, which resulted in American neglect of the country, as well as incompetent and corrupt governance by the government in Kabul and the provinces. After the Taliban seemingly faded away following their embarrassing rout and apparent defeat in late 2001, they came roaring back only a few years later with a new insurgent war plan of guerilla raids and improvised explosive devices (IEDs) that whittle away at the foreign troops.

The ongoing war in Afghanistan is a counterinsurgency effort that was being maintained in early 2010 by General Stanley A. McChrystal, commander of NATO forces in Afghanistan, until he criticized in print his civilian administration in Washington and had to resign. His position as commander was taken over by General David H. Petraeus, who had been regional commander of the U.S. military.

In essence, the counterinsurgency (COIN) doctrine for Afghanistan was that killing insurgent Taliban is counterproductive because their ranks will just be replenished with willing young Taliban troops as long as the people view their government as illegitimate. It is recognized that the more force that is used against the insurgency, the less effective the results. Killing Taliban is no longer seen as an effective way to win the war. In fact, the best weapon in COIN is not to shoot. This is highly frustrating to the mission of the troops brought in to control the violence. In addition, the incompetence and corruption of the Kabul government is legendary, which makes the COIN effort ever more difficult. COIN strategy thus commits the military to civilian goals, particularly with regional development efforts to help the people in outlying areas. Such development is in the hands of the military's Provincial Reconstruction Teams (PRTs) and the Agribusiness Development Teams (ADTs) that have been charged with rebuilding in Afghanistan as the main strategy against Taliban incursions. Human Terrain Systems (HTS) military teams composed of a wide variety of specialists in cultural understanding and development also contribute to the COIN effort.

CHAPTER 6

People and Culture

The cover photograph of the June 1985 edition of *National Geographic* was of a young Afghan woman. Her haunting expression and troubled sea-green eyes told of a life of great hardship. The woman came to be known as the "Afghan girl," and her face became one of the world's best-known images. Yet for 17 years, her name, location, and state of well-being were unknown to the world. She had first been photographed in 1984 in a camp for Afghan refugees located in Pakistan.

Seventeen years later, she appeared again on the cover of the April 2002 *National Geographic*. The original photographer, Steve McCurry, had located her in a remote mountain village near Tora Bora. Then perhaps 28 years old (she did not know her age), her face was aged and weathered. Of their meeting, McCurry said, "She's had a hard life.... So many here share her story." The mystery woman—

People and Culture 85

identified as Sharbat Gula—had survived nearly a quarter century of war.

During this period of turmoil, an estimated 1.5 million lives have been lost. Millions have been injured, and between 3 and 4 million Afghans have become refugees. Much of her country lies in ruin. These are just some of the realities that have hardened, and saddened, Sharbat Gula and nearly all of the 31 million Afghan people.

POPULATION

Afghanistan's population can only be estimated. Millions of people have died as a result of military activity, hunger, or disease. Millions of others have left the country as refugees to neighboring Pakistan or Iran, or elsewhere. Political instability, poverty, and isolated rural populations scattered about the country's rugged landscape make it all but impossible to take a formal census. It is believed that perhaps 31 million people live in the country, with another 4 to 5 million Afghans living as refugees in neighboring countries. Even though much of the country is mountainous or desert land, its population density is estimated to be about 120 people per square mile (46 per square kilometer). In many countries, population density figures are misleading. Whereas the figure is for the country as a whole, huge numbers of people often live in just a few urban centers, leaving much of the rest of the country nearly empty. In Afghanistan, however, only about 20 percent of the people live in cities, leaving nearly 8 out of every 10 scattered around the countryside.

As might be expected in a land ravaged by war, drought, and famine, life expectancy is 44 years—among the shortest in the world. In most countries, women outlive men by a number of years. In Afghanistan, however, men and women have about the same life expectancy. This is one of the few countries in the world where this condition exists. Afghanistan's maternal death rates (death during childbirth) is the world's highest. The same is true of the country's infant mortality rate; 16 percent of all infants die before reaching one year of age. These tragic conditions are the result of inadequate medical care, lack of sanitary facilities (including clean water), chronic hunger, and the harsh life so many women are forced to endure.

Despite the many problems faced by Afghanistan's people, the population continues to grow at an annual rate of about 2.5 percent, more than twice the world average of 1.2 percent. In fact, it is estimated that the country's population will increase by more than a third—to an estimated 39 million—by 2025. But in a troubled land such as today's Afghanistan, these figures are merely speculative. Many elements—including continued conflict, prolonged drought, accelerated rural-to-urban migration, or further integration of women into society through education and employment—can drastically alter rates of population change. The same elements also can influence migration patterns in or out of the country.

In addition to the problems of estimating population numbers expressed here, there is another problem that casts a shadow on population data. Ethnic rivalries and the desire to dominate other ethnic groups also play an important role in population numbers. For example, the warlike Pashtun people, who inhabit much of the east and south of Afghanistan, have ruled the country for many centuries; President Karzai is himself an ethnic Pashtun. The result has been that population numbers are seen as very political, and each ethnic group tries to inflate its size in order to maintain control of as much territory as possible. Another difficulty in estimating Afghanistan's population is the widespread practice of isolating women within a household. Few Afghan males want anyone to know how many women there are in a home. Children are often not counted either; given the high child mortality rates, there is fear that counting them would somehow be bad luck. Thus, Afghanistan has never had a formal census. Perhaps the best census ever conducted was one done in the 1970s. It was based on aerial photographs and satellite imagery of village dwellings, some village interviews, and statistical guesses about the most likely number or people living inside the closed walls.

AN ETHNICALLY DIVIDED LAND

Afghanistan is a country with considerable ethnic diversity, yet few of the ethnic groups live exclusively in Afghanistan. This reality can seriously erode the country's sense of national identity and integrity. For example, Afghanistan's largest ethnic group, the Pashtun, also reside in neighboring Pakistan, and many are more loyal to their "Pashtunistan" ethnic identity than they are to Afghanistan. Tajiks, Uzbeks, Turkmen, and Kyrgyz also reside in adjacent republics that carry their names (the word *stan* associated with so many countries in the region simply means "place of"; *Afghanistan*, for example, means "place of the Afghans"). Much of western Afghanistan is simply a cultural extension of Iran. And the related Baluch reside in the drylands of southern Afghanistan, and also in western Pakistan and southeastern Iran. The Brahui generally inhabit the same areas as the Baluch, widely separated from their relatives in southern India. Other groups include the Nuristani, Kohistani, and Gujar who occupy the rugged mountains of eastern Afghanistan and neighboring countries.

In 2006 the country's largest single group, the Pashtun, made up about 42 percent of the population. Others with significant numbers include Tajik, 27 percent; Hazara, 9 percent; and Uzbek, 9 percent. The small numbers of some 20 other minorities amount to a total of about 13 percent of the population. Many of the ethnic groups, particularly the Pashtuns, are further divided into various tribal units. The principal tribal divisions of the Pashtuns are the Durrani, found chiefly in southern Afghanistan, and the Ghilzai of eastern Afghanistan. Sharp divisions along ethnic and tribal lines are one of the greatest problems Afghanistan faces. It is difficult to politically unify such a culturally diverse people.

Pashtun men wait in line to vote during the parliamentary elections in Kabul in 2010.

LANGUAGE

Language is perhaps the single most important element that binds people together as ethnic groups. A society that is able to communicate among its members is more apt to share common ideas, values, information, views, goals, and other traits. As is amply illustrated by so many ongoing conflicts in the world today, a society divided by language can be difficult to unify. Language differences pose yet another problem for Afghanistan as it works toward integrating all its diverse population into a socially unified state. Four major language families are represented in Afghanistan: Indo-European, Altaic, Dravidian, and Afro-Asiatic (Semitic). A language family is a major language group that, through time, may have branched into many different, yet distantly related, languages. Most languages spanning an area extending from Western Europe to Hindi-speaking India, for example, fall into the Indo-European family.

Afghanistan's two most widely spoken languages, Dari (Afghan Farsi or Persian) and Pashtu are Indo-European. Both serve as "official" languages. Dari, spoken by nearly half of the country's people, serves as a lingua franca—a language most commonly used in commerce and the media and spoken in common by people who otherwise speak their own language. Pashtu is spoken by about 40 percent of the population and Turkic by an estimated 11 percent. The remaining 4 percent of the population is divided among some 30 other languages, a fact that spotlights the country's linguistic diversity.

RELIGION

Formal religious systems have varied considerably through time in Afghanistan. In the past, the area was heavily influenced by shamanistic traditions, many of which still influence Afghan society. Shamanism is a folk religious tradition that is carried out under the leadership of a shaman. This is particularly true of isolated societies in the mountainous Hindu Kush region. This area of Central Asia gave birth to several religious traditions. Among them is Zoroastrianism, which may have developed in Afghanistan between 1800 and 800 B.C. This faith—with its dualistic traditions, such as good and evil and angels and devils—significantly influenced Judaism, Greek thought, and Christianity, as well as religious systems elsewhere in Asia. Zoroastrianism served as the state religion during the seventh-century Sassanian period.

Hinduism may have reached Afghanistan over the trade routes from the east some time during the third century B.C. Today, some 20,000 Hindus live in Afghanistan. Buddhism also became an important religion here. It was introduced during the first century A.D. There is reason to believe that Judaism entered Afghanistan early in the first millennium, and there is still a Jewish presence in the country, although most Jews have immigrated to Israel in recent decades. Most remaining members of this faith live in Kabul, Kandahar, and Herat, where they work as merchants, traders, and moneylenders. By the fifth century, Nestorian Christianity had entered Afghanistan. It soon became the accepted Christian denomination of the Persian Empire. Islam entered Central Asia in the mid-seventh century and rapidly became the dominant religion in Afghanistan and throughout the rest of the region. Today, about 80 percent of the Afghan Muslims follow Sunni Islam, while 19 percent are adherents of Shia sects, particularly the Hazara minority in the central highlands. Finally, there has long been a resident Sikh population—a group centered in northern India. They are the most recent religious arrival, and most Sikhs are engaged in commerce.

EDUCATION

The strides made in the 1960s and 1970s with education in Afghanistan were dramatically curtailed by the Soviet invasion of 1979. During the following decade of war, schooling for the millions of refugee children was limited and commonly emphasized religion in the madrassas, or warlike themes in other primitive schools. Under the Taliban in the 1990s, Afghanistan had only about 900,000 young students, and all of these were boys because girls were prohibited from schooling. The ouster of the Taliban in 2001 quickly led to a great and still unmet demand for education at all levels. Today some 6 million students, both boys and girls, attend school, although another 5.3 million children must still wait for the day when they can attend school, because of restrictions caused by limited classrooms, few teachers, and cultural or security limitations.

About half of Afghanistan's 12,000 schools, for example, have no permanent structure to house them. Instead, classes are held in tents or the open air, and books, blackboards, and

Afghan schoolgirls attend class in a tent set up on the outskirts of Kabul. Makeshift schools such as this are not uncommon in Afghanistan, and teachers, books, and other resources are scarce.

writing materials are scarce. In 2008, the Ministry of Education and foreign donors built about 1,500 schools, and plans are underway for building a similar number annually for the next decade in order to meet demand. Most people realize that education is the only way to overcome the many great hurdles that Afghanistan must still deal with if it is to have a normal existence in the world.

LIVING IN AFGHANISTAN TODAY

With so many social, ethnic, and cultural aspects of Afghanistan in disarray, the nuclear family once again is the most important social unit. Afghan families are very tightly knit. Extended families or clans are also extremely important. During periods of social upheaval, ethnic affiliation becomes increasingly important to people. In other words, when people are under extreme stress, they look inward. They seek comfort and protection—and an essential sense of belonging—within the smallest social units with which they identify.

Over the decades since the Soviet military offensive in the late 1970s, life has been extremely difficult for the Afghans. The human toll as measured by loss of life and limb has been staggering. Families have been fragmented, and interpersonal and interethnic relations have been seriously eroded. The U.S.-led military action that began late in 2001 has further disrupted Afghan society. As was true during the decade of Soviet involvement in the country, it has been accompanied by the introduction of social and economic values incompatible with those of many Afghans.

Life in Afghanistan today is marked by hardship. Families have had to develop coping strategies to survive. Some send sons into combat. Others send family members to other countries to find work, so they can send money to the family left behind. Above all, they hope to protect their children from harm and simply make ends meet in terms of day-to-day survival. No country in the world has more households headed by women, or men crippled by warfare, than does Afghanistan. This circumstance increases family vulnerability in a society that is becoming ever more disoriented. Some relief has been experienced by Westernized, urban Afghans able to again enjoy Western entertainment, other forms of recreation, and less-restrictive interpersonal relations. However, for the vast majority of Afghans—those who adhere to more traditional values—the present is challenging and the future uncertain.

CHAPTER 7

Afghanistan's Government and Economy

In Afghanistan, as is true of many other countries throughout the world, government and economy are closely linked. A strong, stable government with a minimum of corruption and a strong military creates an environment in which an economy can thrive and a country's people can prosper. When government is weak and corrupt and a country is constantly in turmoil, its economy will almost certainly fail. Not surprisingly, considering its recent history of corruption and violence, Afghans today rank among the world's poorest people.

GOVERNMENT

During the twentieth century, the design of Afghanistan's official flag changed nearly 20 times. Conflict among different groups over the most appropriate symbol to represent the country—the design of its flag—is just one example that illustrates the political instability that has plagued the country throughout most of its history. Afghanistan has experienced a dizzying flow of different governments over the years.

It is believed that the tribal societies of ancient Afghanistan were governed much as they are today. Leadership was provided by headmen, councils of elders, and perhaps shamans, or religious leaders. Throughout Afghan history, multiple systems of governance have coexisted.

As is true in the United States, some political decisions have been and continue to be made at a local level. In Afghanistan, such decisions were usually tribal in nature. Above this level, there was generally a hierarchy in which one or more systems were dominant. In part, the plural nature of governance reflected Afghanistan's distance from centers of power. For example, the highest level of authority during much of the country's early history was in the hands of powerful, distant countries. Because they were remote, their power often was limited and considerable freedom was permitted with regard to local government.

During the early years of Islamic expansion, Afghanistan was still somewhat remote from the centers of power. This situation, however, soon changed. Different levels of governance do continue to exist in Afghanistan's predominantly Islamic society. But Islam is much more rigid than most other religious systems—the religion itself strongly influences how people are governed. Therefore, not only religious beliefs but also social and economic activities are strongly influenced by Islam. And the way people are governed under Islamic laws tends to be much more uniform than in the past. This is the case despite the presence of varying Islamic sects and schools of law.

Recent years have witnessed a struggle between secular (not tied to religion) and religious governance. The formation of an independent Afghan government began when Great

Afghanistan's Government and Economy

Britain relinquished control over Afghanistan's foreign affairs. That date, August 19, 1919, is still recognized as the country's Independence Day. In 1926 King Amanullah visited Europe and countries of the eastern Mediterranean. He was greatly impressed by what he saw and attempted to apply his vision of modernization to Afghanistan. His efforts, however, were strongly rejected by a council of traditional leaders. Since that time—nearly a century ago—there has been an almost constant struggle between religious beliefs, government, and society. Some people and governments want to liberalize society and make government more secular. On the other hand, there are many people who resist change. They prefer to maintain a traditional way of life and want to retain systems of society and governance directed by Islamic laws. The traditional approach was that taken by the Taliban. When they came to power in the mid-1990s, they referred to Afghanistan as the "Islamic Emirate of Afghanistan." This tie between country and religious faith was an echo of the powerful emirates of the country's Islamic past. It was also the foundation for what they hoped would become a modern caliphate—a state under Islamic rule.

Following the defeat of the Taliban, United Nations-sponsored negotiations in late 2001 resulted in the creation of an interim government headed by Hamid Karzai, a much-respected Pashtun leader. The International Security Assistance Force (ISAF) was established by foreign donor governments to keep the peace, as well as to protect government leaders. In 2002, the deposed king Zahir Shah returned to Afghanistan for the first time in three decades. He served a symbolic role, indicating a new stability. A new constitution was ratified in 2004 that created a strong presidency, a two-chamber legislature, and an independent judiciary. Islam was recognized as the preeminent religion, but other religions were protected. Equal rights for women and minority language rights were also guaranteed. In 2004 Hamid Karzai became Afghanistan's first democratically elected president, and in late 2005 the first National Assembly was inaugurated.

The parliamentary election of 2005 resulted in an unfortunate, although not unforeseen, victory for Islamic conservatives and jihadi fighters who had been involved in Afghanistan's seemingly interminable wars of the previous decades. About one-half of the 249-seat Walesi Jirga (lower house of Parliament) is represented by such people, including four Taliban commanders. Only about 50 of the men elected fell into the broad category of educated professionals or independents, and 11 of the new representatives were former communists. Women were constitutionally guaranteed at least 25 percent of the representation and managed to take 68 seats, or slightly more than assured. A popular 26-year-old female candidate, Malalai Joya, had become famous at the first *loya jirga*, or "town meeting" tribal assembly in 2002. She had denounced as criminals the powerful commanders and jihadi leaders who had so traumatized and destroyed the country over the previous two decades. She came in second in her home province of Farah in the southwest of the country, with 7.3 percent of the vote. At least six other women also won seats on their own, without the need for a quota system. It has been hoped that women will have a moderating influence on what certainly could be a sharply divided Parliament.

President Hamid Karzai was able to force through most legislative bills and make ministerial appointments. His fellow Pashtuns, from whom he gained considerable support, controlled more than one hundred seats in Parliament, and he also initially had backing from the educated professionals and some of the independents. One of the most outspoken, educated independents to gain office was Dr. Ramazan Bashardost. A native of Ghazni Province in east-central Afghanistan, he became a vociferous critic of both governmental corruption and the lack of accountability. His chief concern was the way in which billions of dollars of international aid—designed to

Afghanistan's Government and Economy

rebuild Afghanistan—had been mismanaged. Many Afghans are upset over the slowness of reconstruction and the corruption that is so widespread throughout the country. This disappointment may have been translated into votes for Bashardost and other reform candidates.

Afghanistan suffers from past wars, pervasive killings, political corruption, tribal and regional fragmentation, and rampant greed. The democratic elections of 2004 provided a sense of hope for future stability to its residents. Unfortunately, however, the highly flawed elections of 2009, with ballot-box stuffing by all sides, intimidation by Taliban against voting at all, low voter turnout, and other problems cast a pall over the results. The country's Parliament is highly contentious and may easily become deadlocked, and declining attention from an economically and militarily thinly spread U.S. government could signal a decline in post–9/11 rebuilding programs. If reconstruction stalls and too much money continues to be siphoned off by unchecked corruption within the government of Afghanistan as well as among the contractors and within some U.S. government agencies, conditions may revert to prewar levels of chaos. Despite such problems, Afghanistan's physical and human resource base may yet be sufficient to pull the country out of its long-violent and ineffective past. Only time will tell.

As of 2011, the central government was unable to gain control of vast regions of the country and continued to depend upon military forces to maintain even a small amount of control. Separate ethnic factions effectively governed the various parts of the country, and all factions had agreed to follow sharia, or Islamic law. Afghanistan's many political parties essentially reflected ethnic units and relationships. The country's 34 provinces continued to provide the formal framework for political activity.

Today, agencies of the United Nations are playing particularly important roles in their attempt to bring stability to the country and to help its people survive these trying times. Since the Taliban was ousted, Afghanistan has received more than U.S. $4 billion in aid. Sadly, it can be argued that far too much of it has been used to pay foreign advisers or was lost to corruption, and not nearly enough financed actual reconstruction. Several new organizations, however, such as Action Aid and Afghan Aid, are coordinating donations, projects, and programs. With their direction, it is hoped that the approximately one thousand foreign NGOs now operating in the country will be able to boost reconstruction.

THE AFGHANISTAN MILITARY

A major key to the future of Afghanistan is the reconstruction of its military so that peace, once established, can be maintained. The Afghan military has existed since the early 1700s. Following many wars with Persia and India, the modern military emerged in the nineteenth century. In the twentieth century, some upgrading and modernization was accomplished. In the late 1970s and 1980s, the military's capability was spread thin fighting against both the Soviet forces and U.S.-backed mujahideen warriors who resisted the communist government. By 1992, Afghanistan's military had become largely dysfunctional. It had dissolved into various militia groups controlled by different warlord factions largely based upon ethnicity. No vision of a single country to be supported by a national military existed anymore. After the rise of the Taliban in the 1990s the use of military force was established only on the basis of Islamic sharia law.

In the decade since 2001, the Afghanistan military has been reformed by the international community so that it can help knit the country back together. Although problems have occurred in recruitment, training, and paying a reasonable living wage, enough progress has been made so that by 2007 some independent operations apart from the U.S.-NATO ISAF were possible.

Afghanistan's Government and Economy

At the present time the country's military comprises the Afghan National Army (ANA), the Afghan National Army Air Corps (formerly the Afghan Air Force), the Afghan National Police, the Afghan Border Police, and a number of scattered authorized militias. In early 2010, the ANA numbered 108,000 soldiers, with plans to reach 260,000 by 2014, and 400,000 sometime after that. These figures compare to mid-2010 foreign troop strength of 94,000 U.S. military personnel and 48,000 allied forces in the country.

Trained primarily by the United States and under the supervision of American or NATO personnel, the ANA was organized into 31 *kandaks*, or battalions, of 600 people each. The National Military of Academy of Afghanistan was built along West Point lines to provide future military officers, the first class of which graduated in January 2009.

Afghanistan's military faces many problems. Ongoing issues include massive corruption, widespread illiteracy, vanishing supplies, and lack of discipline. In 2010, only about 14 percent of new recruits were literate, which left most unable to read simple instructions for their weapons, a map, or a road sign. Courses in basic literacy to about a third-grade level helped recruits who never had electricity, running water, or even toilets in their homes, or a school to attend as children. Natural tendencies are to divide along ethnic lines, which has to be overcome by a strong push to mix the recruits so that an Afghanistan-first discipline emerges. As of 2010, the ANA was about 43 percent Pashtun, 32 percent Tajik, 12 percent Hazara, and 10 percent Uzbek, with the remaining 3 percent made up of other ethnic groups. A major problem in both the ANA and, especially, the police has been low pay or even a complete lack of pay. In December 2009, the United States doubled the pay of new Afghan soldiers to $140 per month, with a bonus if they served in volatile provinces such as the Helmand. This amount is comparable to what the Taliban insurgency pays its forces.

Afghan National Army soldiers are shown here in 2010. The ANA is one branch of Afghanistan's military, which is committed to strengthening its forces in an effort to aid in stabilization of the country.

ECONOMY

Afghanistan's earliest economy was based on hunting and gathering. It was the ancient people of this region, however, who were among the first to domesticate plants and engage in cultivation. Some archaeologists note that Afghanistan has a number of strains of wild wheat, which is an indicator that this exceptionally valuable plant may have been first domesticated here. In addition to the rain-fed cultivation of cereals, such as barley and wheat, southeastern Afghanistan was closely linked to one of the world's earliest irrigation civilizations—the high culture that arose on the fertile floodplains of the Indus River Valley.

Afghanistan was also an area where early animal domestication took place. Village-based livestock systems were joined

Afghanistan's Government and Economy

by systems of pastoral nomadism when Aryans arrived in the region as early as the second millennium B.C. Traditional systems of cultivation and pastoral nomadism continue to be very important to Afghanistan's economy and millions of its rural people. Today, however, the traditional systems of farming increasingly compete with modern irrigation projects in both northern and southern Afghanistan, and the number of people and herds following the wandering way of life of the pastoral nomad is in sharp decline.

Much of Afghanistan receives scant precipitation and has rugged terrain. Considering its physical terrain, it is little wonder that only about 12 percent of the country is suited to farming. Although barley and wheat remain the principal cereals, they have been joined by corn (maize), millet, rice, and rye. Many types of fruit are grown, including apples, apricots, cherries, dates, figs, and grapes. Pomegranates grow particularly well and are increasingly a valuable export. Afghan grapes and melons also are exported to markets throughout southern Asia. In warmer southern parts of the country, even bananas are grown. Several varieties of nuts also thrive, including almonds, pistachios, and walnuts, although many of the valuable nut trees were cut down for firewood during the last 30 years of war. Garden crops are important to a people who do not have the luxury of purchasing their food from supermarkets. Asparagus, beans, beets, Brussels sprouts, and cabbage are found in nearly every home garden; so are carrots, cucumbers, mustard, onions, potatoes, and pumpkins.

Still other important crops include varieties of hay, particularly alfalfa and clover, used in feeding livestock, as well as cotton, sugarcane, and tobacco. One important crop that has become an integral part of the nation's gross domestic product (GDP) is the opium poppy—the source of the powerful narcotics heroin. The Taliban once briefly banned the planting of opium poppies (it is thought to enable the price to rise), but since the removal of the Taliban by U.S. forces, opium has again become an important crop. In 2006, opium production was 40 percent higher than its 2005 total of 4,500 tons. This upward trend has been steadily increasing in recent years until the troop surge in 2010 diminished production somewhat. In spite of strong attempts by the central government to reduce production, Afghanistan produces nearly 90 percent of the world supply of heroin.

Livestock include cattle, sheep, goats, donkeys, horses, and camels. Fowl such as chickens, ducks, and geese are also kept. Afghanistan is famous for its high-grade karakul (a variety of sheep) pelts. Wool and mutton are also important exports.

Afghanistan has a variety of mineral resources. Its energy resources include coal, natural gas, and some petroleum. Recent investigations by the U.S. Geological Survey have shown that Afghanistan has 3 times more undiscovered or undrilled gas than previously thought and 18 times as much undiscovered oil. The country also has reserves of copper, iron ore, lead, and zinc. The World Bank estimated that the main copper deposit at Aynak was sufficient to capture 2 percent of the world market, and the country also has a world-class iron deposit. A recent bid by China on the Aynak copper deposit was for $3.5 billion, which is the largest foreign-aid project in Afghanistan's history. Unfortunately, mining operations have yet to tap these valuable mineral deposits. At the present time, in fact, no metal mines are in operation and only very limited hydrocarbon production is underway. The U.S. Geological Survey has, however, been assigned the task of redeveloping geological exploration and development in the country, and a number of important new studies have been undertaken. Emphasis was placed on assessments of mineral, coal, and water resources, as well as on training and infrastructure development. Recent ground and aerial exploration has shown a wealth of rare earth sources (such as lithium and other unusual elements) that are critical to modern technology, including cell phones and computers.

Afghanistan's Government and Economy

Afghanistan also has a great variety of precious and semi-precious gemstones, including emeralds that are among the best in the world. The famous electric blue lapis lazuli stone has been exported from Afghanistan for more than five millennia. Carved specimens of it have been found in tombs of the Egyptian pharaohs. Many people believe that Afghanistan possesses a vast amount of undeveloped—and perhaps as yet undiscovered—mineral wealth. In 2010 the U.S. Geological Survey and the Pentagon estimated that the country has as much as $3 trillion worth of resources still in the ground.

Most of Afghanistan's industrial products are based upon the country's agricultural and natural resources. From its livestock come carpets, foods, shoes, soap, and textiles. Processed foods come from both livestock and crops. Furniture is made from wood harvested from the country's ever-diminishing forests and using leather from animal hides. Coal, natural gas, and petroleum are used as energy and also in the manufacture of some products. Cement is produced from limestone and aggregate. Imported copper is worked into various useful items, including containers. In the future, it is likely that Afghanistan will attach growing importance to its role in the further development of Central Asia's energy and mineral resources.

During recent years, trade between Afghanistan and other countries has suffered. In addition to the disruption caused directly by warfare, the country has lost much of its ability to produce, purchase, or distribute commodities of any kind. Traditionally, its major trading partners have been the countries of the former Soviet Union, Pakistan, and Iran, with lesser amounts of trade devoted to several other Asian countries. Trade with Western industrial countries is quite limited.

Afghanistan has a potential labor force of about 15 million people, nearly 80 percent of whom are engaged in agriculture. A very large problem of any potential workforce in Afghanistan is that more than two decades of war has severely limited educational opportunities. This has left a generation of gunmen with few, if any, other skills. Unemployment is around 35 to 40 percent. Only about 10 percent of the people are employed in industry—a figure that ranks very low among the world's nations. A scant 10 percent of the population is involved in construction or commerce. If the war-torn country stabilizes and international aid is received to rebuild, the construction sector of the economy is sure to experience huge future growth. Finally, about 10 percent of the population is engaged in services and other occupations, making this sector of the economy one of the weakest among the world's nations.

Decades of violence and years of drought have combined to severely reduce agricultural productivity. Many Afghan people face hunger, and some regions are experiencing famine as a result of ongoing war-induced disruption of agriculture. The growing of drug-producing opium poppies—outlawed by the now-deposed Taliban—is widespread and amounts to an estimated one-third of the GDP. It is the country's single largest export. The illegal narcotics derived from the plant have high value in the world market. With the lack of central government control and no taxation, many farmers grow poppies. They seek to compensate for the loss of other crops to drought, danger imposed by the enormous number of land mines in rural areas, and continued armed conflict. Poppies are quite hardy under drought conditions and are very profitable to an extremely poor people who have few other means to support themselves. The profit-margin difference between growing wheat and growing opium is 50 to 100 times, which creates a huge incentive to take the risk. Farmers usually lack money to pay for seeds or other agricultural needs, so funds for opium-poppy production are advanced by middlemen and warlords to whom the crop is delivered or sold once harvested. Some substitutions of other high-value crops have been tried with some success in recent years. They include cotton, grapes, and pomegranates.

Periodic attempts have been made by the government and foreign troops to eradicate poppies after the flowers have

Afghanistan's Government and Economy

A farmer tends to a poppy field in Marjah. Forces from the United States, Afghanistan, and NATO were instructed to seize large opium stashes but to leave farmers' poppy fields alone.

bloomed, but this only drives the poor, deeply indebted farmers further into the embrace of the middlemen, warlords, drug smugglers, and the Taliban, who fund the opium production. One possible solution to the problem is to buy the crop and turn it into cheap (and legal) pharmaceuticals. Unfortunately, this idea has been opposed by some countries (for example, India, Turkey, and Australia) that already do this legally. Buying the crop and just burning it is also a possible solution to the problem, but it has not yet been attempted.

Afghanistan's economy has improved considerably since 2002. Billions of dollars in foreign aid and other investments have been received. Thousands of Afghans living in foreign lands send remittances to families still living at home. Currently, Afghanistan exports some $500 to $600 billion of goods annually. Its main export partners are India and Pakistan, which take about half of the country's exports, followed by the U.S. which receives about 20 percent. Today, only about 4 percent of Afghanistan's exports still go north of the border to Russia.

Historically, information about Afghanistan's economy is scant and unreliable, and estimates vary greatly. The country embarked on a modest economic development plan in the 1930s. It founded banks, schools, and a university, and by the 1950s began a series of development plans. By the 1970s these had achieved only mixed results, due to inadequate planning, low educational standards, and shortages of skilled managers and technicians. Following the Soviet invasion of 1979, three decades of war, chaos, and a nearly collapsed educational system either destroyed the limited infrastructure or allowed its remnants to decay further. The GDP has fallen substantially since the 1980s because of the disruption of transport and trade, as well as the loss of labor and capital resources. Since 2001 some economic growth has occurred, mainly because of international aid and a decline of drought conditions.

By 2006 the country's GDP was about $21.5 billion, but by 2008 it had plummeted to $10.6 billion, a drop of more than 50 percent. In 2006 roughly 38 percent of the GDP was derived from agricultural production, but by 2010 that number was down to about 30 percent Another 25 percent has come from industry over the past five years, and about 45 percent is gained from a variety of services. In recent years the annual per capita income has been estimated to be about $800. The country's economy continues to struggle and remains one of the world's poorest. This is very unfortunate for a country that offers so much potential, both in terms of its natural and human resources.

CORRUPTION

All societies have people who cheat. Because the people of Afghanistan have always been so poor, centuries ago a tradition developed of asking for and giving *baksheesh*, or bribes. Even in simple shopkeeping, a little "extra" can be part of the bargaining process in settling on a fair price. The result has been development of a culture of corruption, major and minor, at almost all levels. Corruption in Afghanistan, however, has been defined as "the abuse of public position for private gain." As such, it poses a significant and growing problem across the country, one that undermines security, state and democracy building, and development.

The domestic and international consensus on Afghanistan is that corruption is pervasive, entrenched, and systemic, and by all accounts has now reached an unprecedented level. This view is apparent in the country's dismal ranking in the Transparency International Corruption Perception Index, which, in 2008, ranked Afghanistan 176 out of 180 countries, making it the world's fifth most corrupt country. The reason, of course, was that so much money was pouring into the country to try to overcome the effects of the increasing Taliban-induced violence. A "Wild West" environment contributed to a growing attitude of graft, bribes, and payoffs that grew into the present free-for-all of corruption. Many observers believe that the 2009 election ballot box stuffing was simply the Karzai government's attempt to preserve its hold on the moneymaking apparatus that the government had become. Reforming a system so corrupt at all levels certainly is one of Afghanistan's greatest and most difficult challenges.

After the fall of the Taliban government in 2001, corruption in Afghanistan expanded. More than just the standard-issue bribery, nepotism, and extortion in government, corruption became a whole system in its own right. Networks of corrupt practices and people reached across the whole of government. These networks ensured that the guilty were not brought to justice; commonly the officials and agencies that were supposed to be part of the solution to corruption were major contributors to it. Over and over, reports have noted the failure of the Afghan National Police (ANP), the Attorney General's Office (AGO), and the court system to detect, prosecute, judge, or punish corruption at any level. Even simple travel by vehicle through an area results in being stopped by police with their hands out for a simple payoff before one is allowed to proceed.

The so-called Azimi report was the high-level product of the Inter-Institutional Commission on Corruption chaired by the Chief Justice of the Afghanistan Supreme Court. It serves as the national anticorruption strategy for the Afghanistan National Development Strategy (ANDS). The report explains that the "normal" sources and forms of corruption are related to:

> weak institutional capacity of public administration; weak legislative and regulatory framework as well as weak enforcement of the laws and regulations; poor and/or non-merit based qualifications of public officials; low salaries of public servants; dysfunctional justice sector and insufficient law enforcement; the discretionary power of public administration; and the lack of complaint mechanisms and systems for public scrutiny and illegal profits through opium trade and cross border smuggling.

The sources of corruption specific to Afghanistan are the very large opium economy, which is widely considered to be the most important source of corruption in the country, and the large informal economy; the unprecedented large inflow of international assistance and the pressures to commit development aid quickly also carry associated vulnerabilities to corruption.

Corruption has significantly weakened the educational system that is so fundamentally important to democracy and state building in Afghanistan. Issues have erupted regarding "ghost" employees, work disincentives (inadequate salaries drive teachers to focus more on private tutoring), bribes for grades, teacher competency/performance evaluation, and payment of salaries. Corrupt practices worsen at higher levels in the public system, where university degrees can be bought, often after students first must buy their way in and through their courses.

Although Afghanistan is a large country, arable land is scarce. For rural populations, land is wealth—especially irrigated farmland. As in most countries, housing and land are recognized as a main path to prosperity. Thirty years of conflict and displacement have left the cadastral, or land-registration, systems in tatters, and land is susceptible to grabbing by force, through phony paperwork, or by bribe-paying businesses or local leaders. The informal *shura/jirga* system offers some resolution potential at the village level, but the domination of elite interests may make these practices capable of being subverted. The weak land-registration system hurts family security and inhibits economic growth.

Corruption affects any significant development potential in the country for natural-resource extraction. Afghanistan has substantial undeveloped geological resources of many types. Developing these resources is important if the country is to move ahead economically. This is especially true in regard to ways that promote the creation and expansion of associated infrastructure such as water, smelters, refineries, roads, and schools. Such development should provide for substantial economic growth, employment expansion, increased tax revenues, and business growth. The one major deal to date, the $3.5 billion bid with People's Republic of China to develop the world's largest source of copper in the Aynak mine, is clouded by allegations of massive corruption. The government of Afghanistan lacks transparent and accountable processes to guide decision making on these developments, which opens the potential for more corruption. In addition, the revenues from these deals must be tracked in future transactions.

As an Islamic society, Afghans condemn bribe giving or taking on moral grounds as being contrary to their faith. This general view is moderated, however, by a widespread understanding that survival strategies of low-level public officials require additional funds beyond their small salaries, and that the poor, weak clients may have no alternative other than to give a small bribe. Surveys show that both civil servants and the general public share these views but sharply condemn grand corruption by higher-level officials, who are justifiably viewed as being greedy and excessive. Also condemned are bribes demanded by networks that link commanders, officials, and criminals. This is a huge problem that hinders economic progress in Afghanistan.

Afghans have particular contempt for corruption related to the judicial system, the police, and the hiring and promotion of government employees. The justice sector is widely perceived as the most corrupt system in the country. Many Afghans note that justice is a market commodity to be bought and sold, which is particularly troublesome in a society that values justice and honor. The formal justice system of the police, criminal investigators, prosecutors, and judges has numerous points of vulnerability to corruption that are taken advantage of by officials and citizens. Unfortunately in a society with such corrupt systems, supposed "justice" cannot be expected to be too successful in the long run.

Afghans also believe that international assistance is corrupt, due to cost inefficiencies in delivery through international organizations, NGOs, and companies. Afghan perceptions of international "corruption" criticize the high pay and overhead for NGOs, contractors, consultants, and advisers as a form of corruption, regardless of whether the applicable rules were followed in contracting by the international community. For its part, the Afghan government views much aid as corrupt simply because the resources are channeled outside the national budget and outside their control. This "external

Afghanistan's Government and Economy

Afghan president Hamid Karzai (left) visits the Peking University in Beijing in 2010. Afghanistan has been working with China to develop a significant copper mine, but the deal may be tainted by corruption.

budget" is a target of criticism, regardless of whether outright corruption is involved. Because a great deal of money in foreign aid is now freely available in Afghanistan, true corruption by part of the community of foreign-aid workers has been reported, only adding to the pervasive problem of corruption.

Corruption in Afghanistan has become a major issue that is increasingly recognized worldwide as one that is capable of completely undermining any possible reconciliation or healing after 30 years of war. At a basic level, there are three main initiatives that must be undertaken:

- building governance capacities in transparency and accountability

- reducing corruption where it directly impacts the people of Afghanistan
- changing the culture of corruption that subverts governance at all levels

A strategy for combating corruption in Afghanistan was suggested in 2009 by the U.S. Agency for International Development (USAID) to include six main principles: (1) establishing a High Office of Oversight, (2) setting up a prevention agenda, (3) establishing an education agenda about corruption, (4) forming an enforcement agenda, (5) adhering to the USAID "Do No Harm" principles to make sure that its own procedures do not contribute, and (6) coordinating between USAID and other U.S. government management and donor services. Only by paying great attention to these issues does Afghanistan have a chance to succeed and become more than the failed state it has been for some time.

Afghanistan Looks Ahead

In spite of all the problems in modern Afghanistan, many new attempts are being made to develop the country. As a result, a spirit of optimism is evident in many quarters. For example, new buildings are springing up, especially in Kabul but also in other cities and outlying areas. The road network in the country is being rebuilt in some places, and in others, entirely new, all-weather roads and bridges are being put in for the first time. More than 14 different banks are operating throughout the country, and foreign-aid donors have established different low- to no-interest-bearing small-business loans. The United Nations and the international donor communities continue to provide considerable humanitarian relief. A key effort is to eliminate some of the 5 to 7 million explosive landmines and estimated 750,000 pieces of unexploded ordnance from areas such as villages, farm fields, and roads.

Since 2001, the international community has pledged $25 billion in aid, but by 2010 had delivered only a little over half of that. Far too much of the external aid is wasted, with vast amounts going to the high salaries, security, and living arrangements for foreign workers. Furthermore, because of the danger of working in the outlying provinces, a disproportionate share of the assistance is being used in Kabul, to the detriment of rural areas.

Kabul, the capital and largest city, is dreadfully gridlocked and teems with millions of refugees from the outlying and often violent countryside. In 2004–2005, a new plan called the "City of Light" was formulated to improve conditions. This plan would rebuild downtown Kabul south of the Kabul River with a new and upgraded infrastructure for domestic water, an entirely new sanitation system, and electrical and information technology. The project would be based upon privately funded developments of mixed-use facilities. Plans include hotels, office buildings, retail malls, outdoor markets, medical facilities, and low-cost housing. Also planned are concert halls, movie theaters, public parks, pedestrian malls, a new Afghanistan National Museum, fountains, new roads, parking and a public transit system. Alternate plans for development of an entirely new adjunct capital city to the southeast of present-day Kabul have also been suggested.

In spite of some advances, the history of Afghanistan suggests that the country will continue to experience a tug-of-war in terms of values. Some people will seek to make the country more modern—to undergo a cultural leap of perhaps a century or more. Those who fear modern ways and their accompanying loss of traditional values and other ways of life will continue to resist change. A major conflict of the twentieth century—that of tradition versus modernization and its accompanying changes—is certain to be a major issue well into the twenty-first century.

Afghanistan was never effectively colonized. Therefore, the country does not need to pass through a painful period

Afghanistan Looks Ahead

Afghan women pray over graves near a newly built residential area in Kabul. Since the fall of the Taliban, Kabul has enjoyed significant reconstruction, but lacks basic infrastructure such as running water, sewers, power, and paved roads.

of decolonization (the process of learning how to function as an independent country). In terms of the future, perhaps neighboring Iran can be looked to as a possible model. That country experienced several major cultural and political revolutions during the last half of the twentieth century. Until 1979 a shah who attempted to modernize the country governed Iran. His often-harsh rule and rapid steps toward modernization caused much dissension. Ultimately, he was forced into exile and replaced by a religious fundamentalist who declared the country to be an Islamic republic subject to Islamic laws. By 1999, however, there were signs that the government of Iran was relaxing many of its rules and beginning to look outward toward the global community. As has happened in Iran, Afghanistan can return to many of its traditional cultural roots, and its society can evolve into one that is stabilized by shared core values. It can address environmental and social issues of importance and can also be more open to collaboration with the West. Although Afghans resisted colonial encroachment and greatly resent the armed intrusions of the Soviets and Americans, they do appreciate Western technology and have historically maintained close ties with the West.

The future of Afghanistan, as well as other Muslim countries, depends heavily upon a better-informed and more understanding and tolerant West. It is particularly important that the United States, as the world's only remaining superpower, reconsider its role on the global stage. The "rights" and "wrongs" of U.S. military involvement in Afghanistan will be debated for decades. Certainly, Americans were outraged by the events of September 11, 2001. Few people would argue whether Osama bin Laden acted as a ruthless terrorist. But in the process of seeking and punishing this one individual with his small group of supporters, too much of a country was laid to waste with little success.

There were no Afghans on the 9/11 terrorist airplanes. This reality has given strong support for Western assistance in reconstructing Afghanistan in the hope of keeping the country out of the hands of future terrorists. Sadly, the reconstruction of Afghanistan had barely begun when U.S. resources and attention were diverted by the country's invasion of Iraq in 2003. Afghans are just as passionate about their freedoms as are Americans. Some observers now believe that had Afghanistan been rebuilt in a robust way and democratic government more strongly promoted, the United States would have achieved much more success in the fight against al Qaeda terrorism than it did by invading Iraq. A resurgence of the Taliban and violence in Afghanistan also seems to be mounting as a result of too few foreign coalition troops to maintain the peace. America's huge budget deficits resulting from ongoing military efforts may ultimately hurt the effort to rebuild Afghanistan. The United States may decide that it can no longer afford to prop up their client regime and leave it to its own devices.

Afghanistan is seen by some as a failing and corrupt experiment in centralized democracy. Some observers believe that the country is perhaps heading toward some sort of partition based on ethnic lines, with the Taliban in control in some areas and unstable, ill-regulated strongman or warlord governance in other regions. The original borders of Afghanistan were entirely a construct of British and Russian imperialism against local Afghan desires in the nineteenth century. There may be no good reason to maintain these borders today. Certainly were Afghanistan to break up politically, this would cause great unease in all the neighboring national capitals because of the danger to their own powers or federations. Instead, a shift toward a decentralized democracy—giving Afghanistan's various ethnic and physically remote regions greater autonomy—may occur as a lesser of several possible solutions. Afghanistan could thus be governed in a number of different ways that would meet core U.S. security interests and place the country on a path toward tolerable stability.

The political future holds many possibilities for Afghanistan. The country could become a centralized democracy, which has been tried recently but is failing to work. It may become a decentralized democracy, a regulated mixture of democratic and nondemocratic territories, or a partitioned collection of ministates of various possible configurations. It could even become an anarchy, such as Somalia, or a centralized dictatorship. This new range of power-sharing models should be thoughtfully considered. It is essential that a solution

Many Afghans appreciate Western technology, which can help in integrating Afghanistan into the global society. Pictured here is a group of twelve teachers who were presented with new computers and printers while they visited the United States.

be found that best meets the needs of Afghanistan's numerous factions and constituencies. The current attempt by outsiders to impose the ideas of democracy on the country and its people is simply not working.

Afghans and other Middle Easterners also think historically, and much of the history they recall is one of manipulation and humiliation by foreign aggressors. Perceived insults and other grievances, as well as access to advanced technology, have bred a new and ominous form of militancy. Its destructive impact has been seen in recent years. The time has come to develop more inclusive systems of international commerce and governance—systems more sensitive to culture and circumstance. Were such a New World Order for Afghanistan to come to pass, Afghans might find fulfillment and security.

If Afghanistan is unable to overcome these obstacles, the country's future is bleak. Its impact on other countries could also then be equally unpleasant. On the other hand, if Afghanistan is able to overcome its many problems—and there are growing signs that this can be accomplished—it has the natural and human resource potential to become a strong and stable country. Time and goodwill from Western and neighboring countries may allow this to happen.

Facts at a Glance

Physical Geography

Location	Southern Asia, north and west of Pakistan, east of Iran
Area	Total: 251,827 square miles (652,230 square kilometers)
Climate and Ecosystem	Arid to semiarid; cold winters and hot summers
Terrain	Mostly rugged mountains; plains in north and southwest
Elevation Extremes	Lowest point is Amu Dar'ya, 846 feet (258 meters); highest point is Nowshak, 24,557 feet (7,485 meters)
Land Use	Arable land, 12.13%; permanent crops, 0.21%; other, 87.66% (2005)
Irrigated Land	16,902 square miles (43,776 square kilometers) (2003)
Natural Hazards	Damaging earthquakes occur in Hindu Kush mountains; flooding; droughts
Environmental Issues	Limited natural freshwater resources; inadequate supplies of potable water; soil degradation; overgrazing; deforestation (much of the remaining forests are being cut down for fuel and building materials); desertification; air and water pollution

People

Population	31,056,997 (July 2006 est.); males, 15,898,475 (2006 est.); females, 15,158,522 (July 2005 est.)
Population Density	120 people per square mile (46 per square kilometer)
Population Growth Rate	2.47% per year (2010 est.)
Net Migration Rate	0.42 migrant(s)/1,000 population (2010 est.)
Fertility Rate	5.5 children born/woman (2010 est.)
Life Expectancy at Birth	Total population: 44.65 years; male, 44.45 years; female, 44.87 years (2010 est.)
Median Age	18 years
Ethnic Groups	Pashtun, 42%; Tajik, 27%; Hazara, 9%; Uzbek, 9%; Aimak, 4%; Turkmen, 3%; Baluch, 2%; other, 4%
Religions	Sunni Muslim, 80%; Shia Muslim, 19%; other, 1%
Literacy	(age 15 and over can read and write) Total population: 36%; male, 51%; female, 21% (1999 est.)
Human Development Index (HDI)	155 among the 169 countries rated

Economy

Currency	Afghani (AFA)

Facts at a Glance

GDP Purchasing Power Parity (PPP)	$23.35 billion (2009 est.)
GDP Per Capita (PPP)	$800 (2009 est.)
Labor Force	15 million (2004 est.)
Unemployment	35% (2008 est.)
Labor Force by Occupation	Agriculture, 78%; industry, 6%; services, 16% (2009 est.)
Industries	Small-scale production of textiles, soap, furniture, shoes, fertilizer, cement; hand-woven carpets; natural gas, coal, copper
Exports	$547 million—not including illicit exports or reexports (2009 est.)
Imports	$5.3 billion (2008 est.)
Leading Trade Partners	*Exports:* India, 23.5%; Pakistan, 17.7%; U.S.A., 16.5%; Tajikistan, 12.8%; Netherlands, 6.9% (2008) *Imports*: Pakistan, 36.5%; U.S., 9.3%; Germany, 7.5%; India, 6.9%; (2008)
Export Commodities	Opium, fruits and nuts, hand-woven carpets, wool, cotton, hides and pelts, precious and semiprecious gems
Import Commodities	Capital goods, food, textiles, petroleum products
Transportation	*Total*: 21,618 miles (34,791 kilometers); paved, 5,115 miles (8,231 kilometers); unpaved, 16,503 miles (26,559 kilometers) (2003); *Airports*: 46,10 paved (2005); *Waterways*: 124 miles (200 kilometers), chiefly Amu Dar'ya, which handles vessels up to 500 DWT (2005)

Government

Country Name	Conventional long form: Islamic Republic of Afghanistan Conventional short form: Afghanistan Local long form: Jomhuri-ye Eslami-ye Afghanistan Local short form: Afghanistan Former: Republic of Afghanistan
Capital City	Kabul
Type of Government	Islamic republic
Head of Government	Hamid Karzai (since December 7, 2004). The president is both the chief of state and head of government; former king Zahir Shah held the honorific "Father of the Country" and presided symbolically over certain occasions, but lacked any governing authority. He died in 2007.

Facts at a Glance

Independence	August 19, 1919, (from UK control over Afghan foreign affairs)
Administrative Divisions	34 provinces

Communications

TV Stations	At least 16, including one government-run central television station in Kabul
Radio Stations	Estimated 50 private and 30 community-based broadcast stations
Telephones	12.3 million (12 million of which are cellular) (2009 est.)
Internet Users	500,000 (2008 est.)

Primary source: *CIA-The World Factbook: Afghanistan* (2010)

History at a Glance

A.D.	
11000	Archaeological evidence indicates the presence of settled agricultural populations in southern Afghanistan.
Fourth Millennium	South-central regions of Afghanistan are intimately associated with the Indus civilization, a relationship that persists into the second millennium B.C.
Sixth century	The kingdoms of Bactria and Sogdiana are established in Afghanistan; the prophet Zoroaster rises to prominence in Bactria; the region is later incorporated into the Achaemenid Empire.
331	Bactria, Sogdiana, and surrounding regions fall to forces of Alexander III of Macedon (Alexander the Great); Greco-Bactrian dominance continues until ca. 130 B.C.
A.D.	
Mid-seventh century	Islam expands into Afghanistan.
Tenth–twelfth centuries	The Ghaznavid Empire, among the most important indigenous Afghan empires, flourishes during this period; it extends from Kurdistan to Kashmir and is known for its patronage of the arts, literature, and science.
Thirteenth century	Invasions by Mongol and Turco-Mongol forces—particularly destructive are the 1220 and 1221 campaigns of Genghis Khan
Sixteenth century	From the sixteenth through the seventeenth century, Afghanistan is contested between the Persian Safavids and Indian Mughals.
Nineteenth century	Great Britain and Russia seek control over Afghanistan in what has become known as the Great Game; Anglo-Afghan wars occur in 1839–1842 and 1878–1880.
1893	The Durand Line separating Afghanistan and British India is drawn through the middle of the Pashtun tribal lands, thus serving as a basis for subsequent conflict between Afghanistan and Pakistan.

History at a Glance

1936	Afghanistan signs a trade agreement with the Soviet Union and a treaty of friendship with the United States.
1964	A constitution providing for a democratic government is drafted, but lack of agreement on its provisions prevents implementation.
1979	Soviets dispatch 85,000 troops to Afghanistan at the request of Prime Minister Amin; he is then assassinated and replaced by Babrak Karmal, a more moderate leader supported by the Soviets; mullahs and khans declare a jihad, and mujahideen guerrillas attack government and Soviet troops.
1988	A peace accord is signed by Afghanistan, Pakistan, the Soviet Union, and the United States.
1994	Conflict increases among ethnic factions; the Taliban capture Kandahar as a first step in their effort to stabilize the country.
1996	The Taliban gain control of Kabul; U.S. support for the Taliban increases.
1999	The United States initiates UN economic sanctions punishing the Taliban for providing sanctuary to Osama bin Laden; discussions regarding a U.S. military offensive against the Taliban government and al Qaeda continue.
2001	Terrorist attacks in the United States attributed to al Qaeda trigger a massive military offensive designed to curb terrorism.
2002	A provisional government is established in Kabul; the military offensive continues.
2004	Hamid Karzai is elected president.
2005	Parliament is elected and the military occupation of Afghanistan by the United States and ISAF continue.
2006	American University of Afghanistan, which provides an English-language, coeducational learning environment, opens.
2007	Former King Zahir Shah dies.
2008	Large numbers of civilian casualties in the anti-Taliban military efforts are condemned by Karzai and public opinion worldwide, while President Bush authorizes a "quiet surge" of American troops.

History at a Glance

2009 Hamid Karzai is reelected president in an election fraught with extensive ballot stuffing by different sides; President Obama escalates the troop surge.

2010 Afghan parliament rejects 17 out of 24 Karzai cabinet appointees while he bizarrely accuses foreign observers of producing election fraud and trying to put a puppet government in place. The number of deaths per month in the ongoing war is the largest ever.

Bibliography

Arberry, A.J. *The Legacy of Persia.* Oxford: Clarendon Press, 1953.

Bergen, Peter L. *Holy War, Inc.: Inside the Secret World of Osama bin Laden.* New York: Free Press, 2001.

Central Intelligence Agency. *The World Factbook—Afghanistan.* Found online at: http://www.cia.gov/cia/publications/factbook/index/html.

Collins, Joseph J. *The Soviet Invasion of Afghanistan: A Study in the Use of Force in Soviet Foreign Policy.* Lexington, Mass.: Lexington Books, 1986.

Department of the Army. *Area Handbook for Afghanistan.* (Pamphlet 550–65, 4th edition). Washington, D.C., 1973.

Douglas, William O. *Beyond the High Himalaya.* Garden City, N.Y.: Doubleday, 1952.

Dupree, Louis. *Afghanistan.* Princeton, N.J.: Princeton University Press, 1973.

Efendi, Evliya. *Narrative of Travels in Europe, Asia, and Africa, in the Seventeenth Century* (Joseph von Hammer, trans.). London: Oriental Translation Fund of Great Britain and Ireland, 1846.

Ehrenreich, Barbara. "Christian Wahhabists." *The Progressive,* January 2002.

Frye, Richard N. *The Heritage of Persia.* Cleveland, Ohio: World Publishing Company, 1963.

Khrushchev, Nikita. *Khrushchev Remembers* (Strobe Talbott, trans. and ed.). London: Andre Deutsch, 1971.

Mackinder, H.J. *Democratic Ideals and Reality.* New York: Henry Holt, 1919.

National Geographic Society. *Afghanistan and Pakistan.* Washington, D.C.: National Geographic Society, December 2001.

Nollau, Gunther, and Hans J. Wiche. *Russia's South Flank.* New York: Praeger, 1963.

Rashid, Ahmed. *Taliban: Militant Islam, Oil and Fundamentalism in Central Asia.* New Haven, Conn.: Yale University Press, 2000.

Shah, Sonia. "Veiled Solidarity." *The Progressive,* January 2002.

Wilber, Donald N. *Afghanistan: Its People, Its Society, Its Culture.* New Haven, Conn.: HRAF Press, 1962.

Further Reading

Bodansky, Yossef. *Bin Laden: The Man Who Declared War on America.* Rocklin, Calif.: Prima Publishing, 1999.

Cohen, Saul B., ed. *The Columbia Gazetteer of the World.* New York: Columbia University Press, 1998, vol. 1.

Ewans, Martin. *Afghanistan: A Short History of Its People and Politics.* New York: Harper Perennial, 2002.

Hopkirk, Peter. *The Great Game: On Secret Service in High Asia.* London: John Murray, 1990.

McEvedy, Colin. The *Penguin Atlas of Medieval History.* Harmondsworth, England: Penguin Books, 1961.

Rasanayagam, Angelo. *Afghanistan: A Modern History.* London: I.B. Tauris, 2005.

Sabini, John. *Islam: A Primer.* Washington, D.C.: Middle East Editorial Associates, 1983.

Textor, Robert B. *Cultural Frontiers of the Peace Corps.* Cambridge, Mass.: MIT Press, 1966.

Web sites

News and Information on Afghanistan
http://www.afghanistan.com/

Information on Afghan Culture, History, Politics, Society, Languages
http://www.afghan-web.com/

Afghanistan: A Country Study
http://lcweb2.loc.gov/frd/cs/aftoc.html

A Life Revealed: The Story of Sharbat Gula
http://magma.nationalgeographic.com/ngm/afghangirl/

Afghanistan
http://travel.nationalgeographic.com/travel/countries/afghanistan-guide/

Picture Credits

page:
- 2: ©Infobase Learning
- 11: ©AFP/Getty Images
- 13: © Infobase Learning
- 18: © Infobase Learning
- 23: © Ric Ergenbright/CORBIS
- 31: © Ric Ergenbright/CORBIS
- 34: © Paul Almasy/CORBIS
- 37: AP Images
- 43: © Bettmann/CORBIS
- 47: © Reuters/CORBIS SABA
- 52: AP Images
- 56: AP Images
- 63: AP Images
- 68: AP Images
- 72: AP Images
- 80: AP Images
- 88: AP Images
- 91: AP Images
- 100: ©AFP/Getty Images
- 105: AP Images
- 111: ©Getty Images
- 115: ©AFP/Getty Images
- 118: Courtesy John F. Shroder

Index

Abbasid Caliphate, 32
Ab-i-Stada Lake, 25
Achaemenid Empire, 12, 30, 32, 35, 38
Action Aid, 98
Afghan Aid, 98
"Afghan girl," 84
Afghan National Army (ANA), 99, 100
Afghan National Police (ANP), 108
Afghan term, 12
Afghanistan (Dupree), 48–50
Afghanistan (Wilber), 71
Afghanistan National Development Strategy (ANDS), 108
Afghanistan National Museum, 114
Agribusiness Development Teams (ADTs), 83
agriculture, 45, 60
    in ancient history, 30, 36–37
    crops, 101–102, 104–105
    disruption of, 104
    irrigation and, 100, 101, 109
    livestock, 100–101, 102, 103
    percent of workforce in, 103
    in prehistory, 29
    soils and, 22
Al Jazeera news channel, 78
al Qaeda
    hatred of Americans, 81
    Operation Enduring Freedom and, 78–79
    Osama bin Laden and, 77–78
    presence in Afghanistan, 73
    U.S. fight against, 116–117
Alexander the Great, 8, 20, 32, 82
Alpine-Himalayan mountain belt, 17
Amanullah (king), 41–42, 43, 51, 95
Americans
    al Qaeda hatred of, 81
    Communism and, 47
    "humanitarian aid" of, 46
    need for strong allies, 48
    Soviets and, 51
    terrorism against, 14
Amin, Hafizullah, 61–62
Amu Dar'ya (Amu River), 10, 19, 20, 26, 33
ancient history, 29–32
Anglo-Afghan Wars, 39
animals. *See* ecosystems/wildlife
aqueducts, 30–31
"Arab Afghan" allies, 63–64, 81
Arabian Sea, 46, 54
archaeological sites, 28
architecture, 36
Arghandab (river), 20, 21, 44
Attorney General's Office (AGO), 108
Aynak, Afghanistan, 102, 109
Azimi report, 108

Bactra, 37
Bactria, kingdom of, 12, 30, 36, 37
Badakhshan Province, 10

bad-i-sad-u-bist ruz ("wind of 120 days"), 12
Baghlan, Afghanistan, 36
Bajaur, Pakistan, 79
baksheesh (bribes), 107, 110
Balkh, Afghanistan, 34, 35, 37
Baluch people, 25, 87
Baluchistan, 28
Bamiyan Province, 23
Bamiyan Valley, 31
Bashardost, Ramazan, 96
bazaars (markets), 8
Beyond the High Himalaya (Douglas), 9
Bierce, Ambrose, 14
bin Laden, Osama
    in Afghanistan, 76
    al Qaeda and, 77–78
    Iraqi invasion of Kuwait and, 81
    9/11 terrorist attacks and, 116
    Operation Enduring Freedom and, 78–79
    regional unification and, 79
birds, 25–26
Blue Mosque, 72
Brahui, the, 87
bribes (*baksheesh*), 107, 110
Bridas, 75–76
British colonialists, 54
British imperialism, 117
Buddhism, 89
Bush administration, 82

cadastral (land-registration), 109
carpets, 38, 103
Caspian Sea basin, 74
Center for Afghanistan Studies, 75
Central Asia, 13, 14, 29, 33, 39, 48, 74, 75, 80, 89, 90, 103
Central Treaty Organization (CENTO), 47
Chabahar, Iran, 45
chadri. *See under* purdah
China, 13, 14, 26, 33, 62, 102, 109, 111
Christianity, 53, 73, 90
climate, 16
climate change, 16–17
Clinton, Bill, 77
Cold War, 41, 45, 46, 82
collectivization, 48
Collins, Joseph, 57
colonialism, 73
Communism
    containment of, 47
    modernization and, 61, 71
    Muslim clerics and, 50
    political, 49
    retreat of international, 64
constitutional monarchy, 56
constitutional period, 55–59
    Afghan currency and, 57
    Daoud and, 55–56, 58
    Soviet invasion and, 57–58

Index

student protests and, 58–59
corruption, 97, 99, 106–112
    anticorruption strategy and, 108
    "external budget," 110–111
    forms of, 107, 108
    initiatives and, 111–112
    in judicial system, 110
    land registration and, 109
    opium trade and, 108
counterinsurgency (COIN) doctrine, 83
coup d'état, 44, 60
crime, punishment and, 68
crops, 101–102
culture. *See also* West, the
    corruption and, 107, 112
    history and, 27–38
    inclusive systems and, 118
    "inward"/"outward" gender relationships, 53
    irrigation and, 100
    Islamic law and, 67
    people and, 84–92
currency, 57
Curzon, George, 41

Daoud (prime minister), 50, 51, 53, 54, 55
Daoud Khan, Sirdar (Prince) Muhammed
    coup d'état and, 60
    decade of, 45–51
    initiatives of, 57
    Pashtunistan issue and, 53
    as prime minister, 44
    resignation or, 54–55
    return of, 59–60
de Gualle, Charles and Yvonne, 56
decolonization, 115
deforestation, 22, 24
Deh Morasi Ghundai, Afghanistan, 28
democracy, decentralized, 117
Democratic Ideals and Reality (Mackinder), 40–41
demographics, 85–87
    census, lack of, 86–87
    infant mortality rate, 86
    life expectancy, 85
    population growth rate, 86
desertification, 22
deshrubification, 22
diseases, insect-borne, 26
Dostum, 65, 66
Douglas, William O., 9
droughts, 17
Dupree, Louis, 48–50
Durand Line, 44, 54
Durrani Pashtun, 62
dust storms/winds, 11–12

earthquakes, 10, 17, 19
economy, 100–106. *See also* agriculture

foreign trade, 103
improvement in, 105–106
labor force, 103–104
natural resources, 102–103, 109
unemployment, 104
ecosystems/wildlife, 23–26
    animals, 25
    birds, 25–26
    fish, 26
    insects, 26
    types of ecosystems, 24–25
    vegetation and, 23–24, 29
education, 90–91, 106, 108. *See also* madrassas
Efendi, Evliya, 30
Ehrenriech, Barbara, 72–73
Eslam Qal'eh, 21
ethnicity
    divisions and, 86, 87
    military and, 99
    relationships and, 53, 91–92
European imperialism, 39–60, 43
    constitutional period, 59
    Daoud Khan, 45–51, 59–60
    independence, 41
    King Amanullah, 41–42
    Nadir Shah, 42
    overview, 39–41
    purdah and *chadri*, 51–54
European Union, 74–75
Export-Import Bank, 48

Fahd (king), 81
"failed state," 77, 112
family life, 91, 92
famine, 104
Farah Province, 96
Faryab Province, 38
fauna. *See* ecosystems/wildlife
Firdousi, 35
flag design, 93–94
flora. *See* ecosystems/wildlife

gardens, 37–38
garments. *See* purdah
gender roles
    "inward"/"outward" relationships, 53
    public places and, 52
geography. *See* physical landscape
Geoponika, 36
Ghaznavid Emirate, 32
Ghaznavid Empire, 34
Ghazni, Afghanistan, 25, 34, 35
Ghazni Province, 96
Golden Age of Islam, 80
government, 93–98. *See also* Parliament
    flag design and, 93–94
    flawed elections, 97
    inclusive systems of, 118

Index

multiple coexisting systems, 94
theocratic state, 73
Great Britain
    Durand Line and, 40
    independence from, 43, 94–95
    interest in region, 41
    Russia and, 39
Greek (Hellenistic) influences, 32
gross domestic product (GDP), 101, 104, 106
Gula, Sharbat, 85

Hadith, 51
Hadley and Ferrel cells, 17
hamuns (temporary lakes), 16–17
Hanafi sharia, 51
handicrafts, 38, 60
Hari Rud river system, 20, 21
Hari Rud Valley, 8
Hasim, Muhammad, 44
Hazara Muslims, 90
"Heartland Theory," 40
Helmand Province, 99
Helmand River, 10, 12, 19, 21, 44
Helmand Valley Authority (HVA), 44
Helmand-Arghandab river system, 20
Hephthalites, 32
Herat, Afghanistan, 35, 63
Herat Province, 19, 21
hereditary constitutional monarchy, 57
heroin, 101, 102
Hesar Range, 21
Heslin, Sheila, 74
Hindu Kush mountain range
    length of, 19
    Nowshak mountain in, 11
    as primary range, 18
    religious traditions and, 89
    rivers, streams and, 21, 26
    shamanism in, 89
    tunnel through, 46, 47
Hinduism, 89
history, 27–38
    ancient, 29–32
    cultural contributions, 33–38
    early Islamic period, 32–33
    prehistory, 27–29
holy war. *See* jihad
Human Terrain Systems (HTS), 83
humanitarian aid, 46, 75, 113. *See also* international aid
Huntington, Samuel P., 72

illiteracy, 99
improvised explosive devices (IEDs), 82
Inayatullah, 43
independence, 41
Independence Day, 95
India, 41
Indus River Valley, 20, 21, 100
industrialization, 49, 60
infidels (non-Muslims), 35, 61
insects, 26
insurgent war plan, 82
Inter-Institutional Commission on Corruption, 108
international aid, 96–97, 98, 104, 108, 110, 113–114. *See also* humanitarian aid
International Security Assistance Force (ISAF), 95
Iran, 14, 16, 21, 34, 38, 81
    Afghan refugees in, 64, 85
    cultural extension of, 87
    government of, 57, 115–116
    as Islamic republic, 80
    map of, 13, 18
    as trading partner, 103
Iranian chronicles, 12
Iranian kingdoms, 30
Iraq, invasion of, 81, 82, 116, 117
Iron Emir, the, 40
irrigation. *See under* agriculture
Islam, 73. *See also* sharia; Sunni Islam
    arrival of, 38, 52–53, 90
    Communist-sanitized, 49
    Golden Age of, 80
    as preeminent religion, 95
    social, economic activities and, 94
    women and, 51
Islamabad, Pakistan, 76
"Islamic Emirate of Afghanistan," 95
Islamic expansion, 94
Islamic fundamentalists, 71–72, 73
Islamic laws, 68, 115–116. *See also* sharia
Islamic period, early, 32–33
Israel, 49, 81, 90

Jami, 35
jihad (holy war), 61, 62, 79, 96. *See also* mujahideen
Joya, Malalai, 96
Judaism, 89, 90

Kabul, Afghanistan, 19, 20, 35, 39, 48, 67, 90, 112, 113
    assistance used in, 114
    capture of, 70, 75
    climate in, 16
    constitutional period and, 55
    corrupt government of, 82, 83
    independence and, 41
    King Amanullah in, 42
    marketplace in, 52
    mujahideen and, 64–65, 66
    parliamentary elections in, 88
    refugees in, 114
    residential area in, 115
    schools/colleges in, 51, 57, 91
    Soviet troops in, 61, 62

Index

Taliban regime in, 75, 77
UK interests in, 54
Kabul River, 20, 21, 114
Kabul University, 57
Kandahar, Afghanistan, 21, 25
    gardens of, 38
    International Airport, 48
    religious conservatism in, 53
    Soviet invasion and, 62
    as Taliban stronghold, 78
Kandahar Province, 79
Karakoram Himalaya, 17
karez (*qanat*), 8, 30–31, 36
Karmal, Babrak, 59, 62
Kart Emirate, 33
Karzai, Hamid, 86, 111
    ballot-box stuffing and, 107
    as elected president, 95–96
Kenya, 77
Khalq ("Masses") faction of PDPA, 61–62
Khan, Ghengis, 33–34
Khan, Sardar Shah Mahmud, 44, 45
Khash Rud (river), 20
Khayyám, Omar, 35
Khomeini, Ayatollah, 80
Khrushchev, Nikita, 46
Khrushchev Remembers (Khrushchev), 46
Khwarezm, Shahdom of, 33
Khyber Pass, 10, 19–20, 21
Koh-e Baba Range, 19, 21
Kushan nomads, 32
Kuwait, 81
Kyrgyzstan, 87

land features, 17–20
land management, 22
land mines, 104, 113
landlocked Afghanistan, 13, 14
land-registration system, 109
language, 88–89
Lashkar Gah, Afghanistan, 21
literature, 35–36
livestock, 100–101, 102, 103
loya jirga ("town meeting"), 96
loyalty, Afghan concept of, 49
Lydian Empire, 37

Mackinder, Halford, 40, 41
madrassas, 66, 90
Mahayana Buddhism, 33
Mahmud of Ghazni, 34, 35
Marjah, Afghanistan, 21, 105
Marxist government, 63
Marxist-Leninist principles, 59
Masoud, Ahmad Shah, 78
Mauryan Empire, 32
Mawlawiya Dervishes, 34
Mazar-i Sharif, Afghanistan, 68, 72

McChrystal, Stanley A., 82
McCurry, Steve, 84–85
Mecca, Saudi Arabia, 81
Medina, Saudi Arabia, 81
Mediterranean region, 10, 74–75, 95
military, 98–100
    aggression/aggressors, 50
    components of, 99
    kandaks (battalions), 99
    problems faced by, 99
mineral resources, 102
Ministry of Education, 91
modernization, 51, 59
    pace of, 60, 73
    Soviet initiatives in, 55
    Taliban and, 71, 72
    traditionalists and, 58, 114
    vision of, 95
Mohmand, Pakistan, 79
Mongols, 33
Morghab (river), 21
Muhammad (prophet), 32, 51
mujahideen, 60, 62, 63. *See also* jihad
Mundigak, Afghanistan, 28
Musahiban family, 42
Muslims, 90. *See also* Islam
    clerics, 53
    constitution and, 57
    purdah system and, 51

Nadi Ali oasis, 21
Nadir Shah, 42
Namakzar (lake), 30
narcotics, 101–102, 104, 108
National Assembly, 96
National Geographic, 84
National Military of Academy of Afghanistan, 99
National Revolutionary Party, 60
National Security Council, 74
nationalism, 51
natural resources, 109
    gemstones, 103
    minerals, 102
Neolithic (New Stone Age) Revolution, 28
Nestorian Christianity, 90
New York City, 77, 78
nomads/nomadism, 28, 36, 52, 69
    Pashtun, 9, 12, 55
    pastoral, 32, 101
nonalignment, policy of, 60
nongovernmental organizations (NGOs), 82, 98, 110
North Atlantic Treaty Organization (NATO), 47, 82, 99, 105
Northern Alliance, 79
Northwest Frontier Province, 79
Nowshak (mountain), 9–10, 11

Index

Operation Enduring Freedom, 78–79
opium, 101–102, 104–105, 108
Organization of Petroleum Exporting Countries (OPEC), 74
Oxus River of antiquity. *See* Amu Dar'ya

Pakistan, 13, 53, 54
    Afghan refugees in, 64, 85
    bin Laden in, 79
    Pashtun "rebels" in, 50
    as trading partner, 103
Palestine/Palestinians, 50, 81
Pamir Knot, 9, 19
Panjsir River, 26
Parcham ("Flag") faction of PDPA, 61, 62
Parliament, 58, 59. *See also* government
    contentious nature of, 97
    elections for, 88
    Walesi Jirga (lower house), 96
Paropamisus (Selseleh-ye) range, 16
Parthian Empire, 32
Pashtun tribes, 53–54
    migratory routes, 55
    nomadism of, 8, 9, 12, 55
    "rebels" in, 50
    supporting Karzai, 96
    tribal divisions of, 87
    warlike nature of, 86
"Pashtunistan"
    concept of, 44, 45, 46, 53, 60
    crisis, 55
    ethnic identity of, 87
pastoral nomadism, 101
pastoralism, 32
People's Democratic Party of Afghanistan (PDPA), 59, 61
Persian chronicles, 12
Persian Gulf, 46
Peshawar, Pakistan, 20
Peshawar Valley, 21
Petraeus, David H., 82
petroleum politics, 74–77
physical landscape, 9–10, 15–26
    area, 14
    climate, 16
    climate change, 16–17
    deserts, 9, 10, 11, 12, 15, 16, 22, 30, 76
    ecosystems/wildlife, 23–26
    land features, 17–20
    map of Afghanistan, 13
    mountains, 8, 9–10, 11, 15, 16, 17, 18, 19
    semidesert conditions, 23, 24, 25
    soils, 22
    southern Afghanistan, 10
    water features, 20–21
Physicians for Human Rights, 69
poetry, 35–37
Pol-e Khomri, Afghanistan, 36
political instability, 74, 85, 94

poppies. *See* opium
population, 85–87
post–9/11 rebuilding programs, 97, 98
power-sharing models, 117–118
precipitation, 11, 15, 101
prehistory, 27–29
Progressive, 69, 72–73
provinces, 97. *See also* specific province
Provincial Reconstruction Teams (PRTs), 83
purdah (*pardah*)
    and *chadri*, 51–54, 69
    in cities, 68

Qur'an, 51, 66

Raman, Abdur, 39, 40
Rashid, Ahmed, 74
reconstruction, 116
regional unification, 79
religion, 89–90, 94. *See also* Buddhism; Christianity; Islam; Judaism
Religious Police (Munkrat), 70–71
Republic of Afghanistan, establishment of, 60
Revolutionary Association of the Women of Afghanistan, 69
river systems, major, 20
"Roof of the World," 9
ruba'i, 35
Rumi, 34
rural communities
    conservative groups in, 60, 61
    food resources for, 26
    international aid and, 114
    isolation of, 85
    land, wealth and, 109
    land mine risks, 104
    nomadic living, 28, 101
    urban migration and, 86
    water scarcity and, 21
    women in, 69
Russia
    czarist, 39, 40, 46
    exports to, 106
    imperialism of, 117
    petroleum politics and, 74
Russification, 49

Safed Koh Mountains, 10, 19, 78
Saffarid Emirate, 32
Salang Pass, 11
Salang River, 26
Salang Tunnel, 46, 47
Samanid Emirate, 32
Sana'i of Ghazni, 34
sanctions, 81
Sassanian Empire, 32, 89
satrapies (provinces), 12
Saudi Arabia, 81
Saur Revolution, 60

133

Index

Seleucid Empire, 32
September 11, 2001 terrorist attack, 14, 78, 82, 116
Shah, Sonia, 69
Shahdom of Khwarezm, 33
Shahname ("Book of Kings"), 35
Shamanism, 89
sharia (Islamic law), 70, 73, 97
Shia Muslims, 90
Shir Khan, Afghanistan, 46
shura/jirga system, 109
Sikhs, 90
Silk Route, 33
Sistan Basin, 21
Sistan region, 25
socialism, 55, 62
soils, 22, 29
Sorkh Kowtal, 36
Southeast Asia Treaty Organization (SEATO), 47
Soviet Invasion of Afghanistan, The (Collins), 57–58
Soviet invasion/aftermath, 61–83
    aftermath of war, 64–66, 92, 106
    invasion, 62–63
    Taliban and, 66–73
Soviet Republics, former, 13, 14
Soviet Union
    assistance projects, 46, 48
    collapse of, 74
    Daoud Khan and, 45–51
    economic ties with, 54
    modernization and, 55
    relationship with, 60, 92
    as trading partner, 103
    tunnel project with, 47
Soviet-Afghan War, 63
Spin Ghar (Safed Koh or White Mountains), 10, 78, 79. *See also* Tora Bora
Sufi mysticism, 34
Sunni Islam, 51, 68, 90

Tahirid Emirate, 32
Tajikistan, 10, 13, 14, 87
talib, 66
Taliban, 53, 66–73, 75–76, 107
    ancient sites and, 31
    fall of, 49, 73, 95, 98, 115
    Islamic law and, 68
    opium growing outlawed by, 104
    payment of soldiers, 99
    resurgence of, 117
    traditional approach of, 71, 72, 73, 95
    viewpoint of, 79–83
    women and, 70
Tanzania, 77
Tariki, Nur Muhammad, 59, 61
technology, modern, 102, 114, 116, 118
terrorism, 14, 77, 116–117

Timur (Tamerlane), 33
Tora Bora, 78–79. *See also* Spin Ghar (Safed Koh or White Mountains)
trade, foreign, 103
Transparency International Corruption Perception Index, 107
Treaty of Rawalpindi, 41
treaty organizations, 47
tribal societies, 94, 97
Turkestan Mountains, 19
Turkey, 38, 105
Turkmenistan, 10, 13, 14, 16, 87

Unai Pass, 21
United Kingdom, 54
United Nations (UN), 44, 97–98, 113
United States (U.S.)
    ANA training in, 99
    arms, loyalties and, 50
    Communism and, 47
    economic aid from, 57–58
    foreign policy, 49
    government allies of, 79, 82
    HVA and, 44–45
    Israel supported by, 81
    military involvement, 57, 116
    mujahideen support from, 62
    narcotics control by, 105
    Pakistan allied with, 53, 54, 77
    petroleum politics and, 74, 75
    policy making of, 74
    Soviet Union and, 48, 49, 51, 57, 62
    Taliban and, 67, 76, 77
    terrorist attacks upon, 14, 78, 82, 116–117
U.S. Agency for International Development (USAID), 112
U.S. Geological Survey, 102, 103
U.S.-led military action, 92
USS Cole bombing, 77
Uzbekistan, 10, 13, 14, 87

veil. *See* purdah

Wakhan Corridor, 14
"warrior society," 67
watchtowers, ancient, 31
water features, 16–17, 20–21
water resources. *See also karez (qanat)*
    aqueducts and, 30–31
    drinking water, 21, 26, 86
    irrigation and, 100, 101
Waziristan, 79
West, the
    collaboration with, 116
    energy security of, 74
    influences from, 79, 92, 118, 119
Westernized Afghans, 69–70
Wilber, Donald, 71
"Wild West" environment, 107

Index

wildlife. *See* ecosystems/wildlife
winds/dust storms, 11–12
women, 87, 92. *See* also purdah
   equal rights for, 95
   Islam and, 51
   maternal death rates, 85
   in parliament, 96
   traditional role of, 52, 70
   unveiled, 73
woodlands, 23
World Trade Center, 77, 78
World War II, 41, 44, 45, 49

Yeltsin, Boris, 74
Yousuf, Muhammed, 56–57

Zahir, Muhammad, 42, 44–45
Zahir Shah, Muhammad
   Daoud's departure and, 56
   exile of, 59
   return of, 95
Zionists, political, 50
Zoroaster (prophet), 12, 33
Zoroastrianism, 51–52, 89

About the Contributors

JEFFREY A. GRITZNER is the chairman of the Department of Geography, the Asian Studies Program, and the International and Cultural Diversity Cluster at the University of Montana. He coordinates the Montana Geographic Alliance. He has traveled extensively in Afghanistan.

JOHN F. SHRODER JR. is regents professor of geography and geology at the University of Nebraska, Omaha, where he and another faculty member started the nation's only Afghanistan Studies Center in 1972, and where he is now the research coordinator. Shroder is also the codirector of Southwestern Asia (Afghanistan and Pakistan) Regional Center for the GLIMS (Global Land Ice Measurements from Space) Project that is designed to assess snow, ice, and water resources for a chronically drought-torn region with high resolution ASTER satellite imagery. This current project is part of his long-running Atlas of Afghanistan Project that has been collecting data and mapping the country for more than 30 years.

CHARLES F. "FRITZ" GRITZNER is Distinguished Professor Emeritus of Geography at South Dakota State University in Brookings. In 2010, he retired from teaching after a 50-year career in academe. In retirement, Fritz, his wife Yvonne, and their "family" of two Italian greyhounds will remain in South Dakota. He enjoys travel, writing, and sharing his love for geography with readers. As a senior consulting editor and frequent author for Chelsea House Publishers' MODERN WORLD NATIONS, MAJOR WORLD CULTURES, EXTREME ENVIRONMENTS, and GLOBAL CONNECTIONS series, Fritz has a wonderful opportunity to combine each of these "hobbies." Dr. Gritzner has served as both president and executive director of the National Council for Geographic Education (NCGE) and has received the council's highest honor, the George J. Miller Award for Distinguished Service to Geographic Education, as well as numerous other national teaching, service, and research recognitions from the NCGE, the Association of American Geographers, and other organizations.